I0838904

Charter of Christian Freedom

Charter of Christian Freedom

A Layperson's Study Guide
to Paul's Letter to the Galatians

GORDON LINDSEY

WIPF & STOCK · Eugene, Oregon

CHARTER OF CHRISTIAN FREEDOM
A Layperson's Study Guide to Paul's Letter to the Galatians

Copyright © 2017 Gordon Lindsey. All rights reserved. Except for brief quotations in critical publications or reviews, no part of this book may be reproduced in any manner without prior written permission from the publisher. Write: Permissions, Wipf and Stock Publishers, 199 W. 8th Ave., Suite 3, Eugene, OR 97401.

Wipf & Stock
An Imprint of Wipf and Stock Publishers
199 W. 8th Ave., Suite 3
Eugene, OR 97401

www.wipfandstock.com

PAPERBACK ISBN: 978-1-5326-0319-8
HARDCOVER ISBN: 978-1-5326-0321-1
EBOOK ISBN: 978-1-5326-0320-4

Manufactured in the U.S.A.   01/10/17

To

the Logos Discussion Class

of the First Presbyterian Church,

Dallas, Texas—

cherished companions

in our shared journey

of Bible study

Contents

A Preface to Study

SOME LITERARY WORKS RESEMBLE a sumo wrestler. They, like the squat wrestler, are short in length, yet these works carry a lot of intellectual heft. Their thoughts, and even sometimes their very choice of words, deliver a wallop that reverberates down through history.

One such literary work is the letter we are making the object of this study. It is the letter the Apostle Paul wrote to a group of Christian churches in the Roman province of Galatia around the middle of the first century.

It is short. It numbers less than one hundred fifty verses in translation, yet it sparked a spiritual revolution that continues to shape the character of Christianity some two thousand years later. If you think Christianity is a religion all about rituals and rule keeping, the Letter to the Galatians is going to shake up your complacency. We might regard it as Christianity's charter of spiritual freedom.

The letter is, in fact, a kind of polemical pamphlet written in the heat of a serious ecclesiastical controversy. The Paul we meet in it is not a cool, dispassionate scholar writing in his ivory tower. He is a pastor faced with what he considers a serious challenge to the gospel of Jesus Christ. He brings all the white-hot heat of his passion for this gospel to his task of safeguarding its integrity.

This may be one reason why Paul's Letter to the Galatians has been so influential. The ancient church wrote more commentaries on it than on any other letter of the Apostle Paul. Martin Luther once called the letter his Katie von Bora. He thus signaled that the book was as precious to him as his own wife. The letter gave teeth to campaigns in the twentieth century to ordain women.

We will try to tap into the strange, spiritual power of this letter as we pursue our study. That may involve some hard work. Paul uses language and concepts common in his own religious and cultural environment. They are not common in ours, so you may feel you need someone to help translate. I will try my best to do that for you.

If I do that task skillfully, maybe you will find that the words Paul wrote to first-century Christians speak powerfully to twenty-first-century Christians. If that happens, you may also find this letter transforms the way you think and live as a Christian. It did so for me.

HOW THIS BOOK WORKS

I do not intend this study guide to be a scholarly commentary on Galatians. That is one reason I use footnotes sparingly. Instead, I try to serve a different audience, an audience of non-theologically trained readers who may be studying Galatians in a church school class, a small group, or individually. Also, I hope this study guide can be helpful to working pastors who seek to draw upon Galatians in sermon preparation. For all these readers, let me note how my guide works.

In the first chapter, I sketch the crisis that was roiling the churches in Galatia. We need to understand that controversy in order to appreciate the passionate concern Paul shows throughout the letter. I also suggest how the debate in these churches may mirror debates in churches today. That's why this ancient letter remains relevant.

In chapters 2 through 27, we will work our way through Galatians. The letter is, as I said above, a polemical tract. We will try to follow Paul's argument as it unfolds. Here my chief concern is explaining the letter's meaning in its first-century environment.[1]

At five different points in the flow of the book, however, I pause to look at the picture of Christian life that unfolded in Paul's presentation. In these five reflections I focus on theological issues that I think are quite relevant to twenty-first-century Christians. Here is where I spend some time thinking about how Paul's ancient thoughts continue to speak to us today.

A WORD OF THANKS

Before I launch into Galatians, I want to express a word of thanks to two who have contributed to the writing of this book.

First, Dr. John Mulder, former president of Louisville Presbyterian Theological Seminary. Having read of some my other writings on the Bible, Mulder, a close friend, was the first to suggest that I try my hand at writing Bible study guides for laypeople. His encouragement has been a great motivating factor along the way. Thank you, John.

And second, the Logos Discussion Class of the First Presbyterian Church of Dallas, Texas. This particular book started as a series of Bible study discussions that I led with the class several years ago. Class members not only gave me an opportunity to share my Biblical studies with them, but they also kept me on my toes with their perceptive and challenging questions. This book is the fruit of our joint journey in Bible study together. I dedicate it to them with joy and gratitude.

---

1. When I quote the Scripture text, I will be quoting from the New Revised Standard Version translation of the Bible, unless I specify otherwise.

1

Churches in Theological Dissension
An Introduction to the Letter to the Galatians

IF WE ARE TO grasp what is so revolutionary about the Letter to the Galatians, then we must first understand the church crisis that motivated Paul to write the letter. That is also essential to understanding the letter's relevance to church life today. So in this first chapter, I want to sketch out the crisis that so alarmed Paul.

That a crisis alarmed Paul is very clear in the intensely emotional language of the letter. In Galatians we do not find Paul engaged in any low-key academic debate. We encounter Paul at his most passionate. In his eyes, the stakes in the crisis are nothing less than the truth and integrity of the gospel of Jesus Christ.

Paul marshals all of his rhetorical tools in defense of the gospel as he understands it. For example, we will find him a master of rabbinic interpretation of Scripture. He was trained in it before he became a Christian. He also shows himself a master of the allegorical interpretation of Scripture favored by Greek-speaking Jews.

Whatever tools he uses, Paul exhibits a style of vehemence in theological debate that may, at times, shock us. I sometimes question whether it did not set a damaging model for later church history. Yet such vehemence is common when people feel that life-and-death issues are at stake, especially when identity issues are under threat.

So what was it that so alarmed Paul?

WHAT ARE WE TO DO WITH THESE GENTILES?

The crisis in the Galatian churches was an outgrowth of what I consider the greatest turning point in the history of Christianity. It was that moment (probably just a few years after Jesus's death and resurrection) when the Christian community of believers began to accept Gentiles into its membership.

Jesus was a Jew; so were all of his twelve original disciples. The Christian church arose within Judaism. The book of Acts tells us that the early Christian community in Jerusalem worshipped regularly at the Jewish temple. For this community, the Scriptures were the Hebrew Bible (our Old Testament), and these early Christians continued largely to follow Mosaic law (the Torah).

The book of Acts tells us that to the surprise of this early Christian community, Gentiles began to be attracted to the gospel of Jesus Christ (Acts 10). Acts even tells us that it was the Holy Spirit that launched this movement. An angel instructs a God-fearing Roman centurion to invite the apostle Peter to his house to preach the gospel. As a result, Cornelius and his whole household become Christians.

Soon, other Gentiles joined the Christian movement. Acts tells us that a very lively church community came into being in the Greek metropolis of Antioch. It contained believers from both Jewish and Gentile backgrounds. It was there that followers of Jesus first came to be called Christians.

But on what basis was the Christian church to accept these Gentiles into its fellowship? Were they to be accepted as equal members of the church, retaining their Gentile ethnic and cultural identity? Or did these new Gentile believers need to first become Jewish, adopting the identity markers of Jews? By the first century

AD, those markers primarily consisted of circumcision of males, observance of Jewish dietary laws, and the keeping of the Sabbath.

If we read carefully the book of Acts as well as other documents in the New Testament and other Christian writings of that first century, we begin to see that this question provoked a fierce debate in Christian circles. Various theological parties arose in the church and passionately argued their case.

The church sought to settle the debate during a church consultation held in the city of Jerusalem. We don't know exactly the date. It may have been held sometime between AD 45 and 50. Acts 15 describes the consultation and its decision. That decision was that Gentiles would be accepted into the church as Gentiles; they did not need to become Jews first. Jews and Gentiles would be equals in the church, although the consultation's decision-makers asked Gentiles to respect certain Jewish sensibilities.

As in many church debates today, the consultation's decision does not seem to have quelled the dissension at first. Factionalism over the issue continued to trouble the church for some time into the future. Ultimately, the decision that Jews and Gentiles would be equal believers won the ascendancy. It may not have happened, however, until after the Christian community in Jerusalem was erased in the destruction of that city by the Roman armies in AD 70.

That the decision of the Jerusalem consultation did gain the ascendancy was to prove decisive for Christianity. It led, in the long run, to a break between Judaism and Christianity. Christianity had its roots in Judaism (and continued to cherish those roots), but it ceased to be a sect of Judaism. It became an independent religion of its own.

THE BATTLEGROUND IN GALATIA

What we witness in the Letter to the Galatians is a concrete example of how this theological dissension over the status of Gentiles affected a group of churches far from the mother church in Jerusalem.

This theological dissension was roiling life in the newly established Galatian churches. There it was causing great confusion and turmoil among the churches' members. Those members included both Gentiles and probably a good representation of Jewish believers.

Biblical scholars fiercely debate whether the theological dissension in the Galatian churches took place before the Jerusalem consultation or after it. If it took place before, we see how the debate agitated Christian communities far from Jerusalem. If afterwards, then we see how the decisions of the Jerusalem consultation continued to be contested.

I do not want to wade into this scholarly debate. There are strong arguments made on both sides. But, in my opinion, neither side has proved its case conclusively. I don't think this particular scholarly debate over the dating of the letter fundamentally effects how we read the letter.

POSSIBLE THEOLOGICAL POSITIONS IN THE DEBATE IN GALATIA

What is important for our reading of the letter is understanding the crisis that was particularly roiling the Galatian churches. Here we must resort to some speculation, for we glean our understanding of the crisis almost exclusively from Paul's letter.

Paul is not an unbiased, dispassionate reporter. When he reports on what his opponents are saying, he does so with the intention of refuting them. We will never know if he reports their positions accurately, because no writings of his opponents survive. We cannot recreate their position from their own writings. So we must rely on Paul's biased viewpoints.

The following, however, seems to be the situation.

A group of traveling Christian evangelists or teachers was apparently visiting the Galatian churches—churches that the Apostle Paul had evangelized and founded. They were churches in predominantly Greek-speaking, Gentile cities.

Galatia was a Roman province in Asia Minor, or what today we would call central Turkey. The leading city of the province was Ancyra. Today we know it as Ankara, the capital of Turkey. The Romans gave the province the name of Galatia because around 275 BC Celtic war bands migrating out of central Europe conquered the area. The Greeks called these Celtic peoples Keltoi or Galatae; the Roman called them Gauls.

For a while, the war bands wreaked havoc among the Greek cities of Asia Minor. However, both Greek kings and the Romans had largely pacified them. By Paul's day, most of the residents of Galatia were Greek-speaking, living under Roman rule. That's why Paul wrote his letter in Greek. Yet there must have been people in these churches who had Celtic ancestry. They were probably the very first Celtic Christians.

After evangelizing Galatia, Paul moved on to other regions, but he maintained close contact with the churches he founded. He heard, therefore, about new Christian teachers who were visiting and preaching in the Galatian churches.

In their preaching, these evangelists argued that Gentile Christians needed to practice the commandments of the Jewish Torah,[1] especially the practice of circumcision. Hence, for convenience, scholars call this group the Judaizers.

In supporting their preaching, the Judaizers appealed to the Hebrew Scriptures. Many of the Gentile believers were probably not familiar with the Old Testament, so they must have been quite

---

1. Throughout this book, I will use the term *Torah* rather than *Mosaic law*. The Hebrew word *Torah* has several layers of meaning. First, it literally means instruction rather than law, and it includes narrative as well as laws. The Greek translation of the Old Testament, however, used the Greek word *nomos* (the Greek word for *law*) when referring to Torah. So Paul uses the word *nomos* also to refer to Torah.

Second, Torah had a narrow meaning: it referred to the first five books of the Hebrew Bible (Genesis, Exodus, Leviticus, Numbers, and Deuteronomy), which we call the books of Moses. But it also had an expanded meaning: it covered not only the contents of the books of Moses proper, but also the extended Jewish religious tradition (with its laws and customs), which were grounded in those books of Moses. When Paul talks about the law, he generally has this multilayered meaning of Torah in mind.

persuaded by the arguments they heard. As a result, many of the male Galatian Gentile Christians had either been circumcised or were seriously contemplating it. Some of these Gentile Christians may also have begun to adopt Jewish dietary laws.

We don't know whether these traveling evangelists were Jewish Christians (possibly even coming from the mother church in Jerusalem) or whether they were Gentile Christians who had adopted Jewish customs and were now arguing that other Gentile Christians should do so, too.

If they were Jewish Christians, they may have been eager to keep Jewish identity markers alive for a very practical reason. Non-Christian Jews were alarmed that the new Christian movement was threatening the supremacy of the Torah in the life of faith. This fed into some of the Jewish persecution of Christians.

The Judaizing party in the church may have been trying to dampen these outbreaks of persecution by emphasizing that all Christians, including Gentile converts, lived by the Torah. They could then argue that Christianity was no threat to Judaism, because all new Gentile Christians were compelled to recognize the supremacy of the Torah. Thus, they could deflect Jewish persecution away from the church.

If the Judaizers were Gentile Christians, they may have wanted to align themselves with what they thought was the more ancient and august religion of Judaism. We have clear evidence that many Gentiles in this era had a great respect for Judaism as an ancient and morally demanding religion. Many of them attended Jewish synagogues regularly. They were known as God-fearers. These God-fearers provided many converts to the new Christian churches. As they entered into the church, they brought with them the high regard they had for Judaism and its hallowed customs.

A DEBATE OVER WHAT CONSTITUTES THE CHRISTIAN IDENTITY

There were possibly three different arguments that these evangelists/teachers were making. Let's look at each of them in turn, for this will bring greater sharpness to our reading of the Letter to the Galatians.

First, these traveling evangelists may have been saying that if Gentile Christians did not adopt the Jewish customs, indeed the whole of the Jewish Torah, then they were not truly Christian. This argument probably had behind it the assumption that salvation came from the Jews and therefore only Jews could be saved.

Behind this argument lay the deep Jewish conviction of the supremacy of the Jewish Torah in the life of faith. That was a particular conviction of the Pharisee party in Judaism, the very theological tradition in which Paul had been educated in his youth. One of the lessons of the Old Testament was that when Jews neglected the Torah, disaster struck the nation. So the careful observance of the Torah was something more than just a matter of religious devotion. It was an issue of national security.

If this were the argument that these traveling evangelists were espousing, then the debate was over Christian identity—who was truly a Christian and who was not. Could a Gentile truly be a Christian without becoming Jewish?

In this debate, the crucial questions were: What constitutes a Christian? What is it that really makes someone a Christian? Who really is a Christian, and who is not?

This fight may feel familiar. We hear similar debates throughout the Christian church today. Whether it is debate over who's born again and who's not, or whether certain theological opinions are acceptable within the Christian community or not, we Christians fight constantly over issues of Christian identity.

That should not surprise us, as some of the fiercest debates not only in religion but also within our wider society concern who's in and who's out. Identity boundaries are where we human beings tend to fight our fiercest battles.

A DEBATE OVER WHAT CONSTITUTES SPIRITUAL MATURITY

On the other hand, these traveling evangelists visiting the Galatian churches may have been arguing a different position. This is the second possible argument fueling the debate.

This argument is that Gentile Christians needed to adopt the Jewish Torah, not in order to be saved, but in order to be more perfect or mature Christians. In this case, if you as a Gentile Christian aspired to move to a more spiritually elevated or superior position, then you needed to adopt the Jewish customs that were being advocated.

If we accept this argument, then we would be creating a two-tier class system in the church. Some Christians would be more elite than others because they adopted the more rigorous Jewish practices. The line of argument might have gone like this. "We are better or more mature Christians because we live by the rigorous requirements of Jewish law."

This way of thinking would have resonated with many Gentiles. The many mystery cults of the Greek world operated on the premise that there were different stages in the spiritual journey. As people were initiated into the mystery cults, they would proceed through various stages until they reached their most elevated status. One might go through a mystery cult liturgy repeatedly in order to advance to the most elevated stages.

This concept of the spiritual journey also resonates with many Christians today. We sometimes hear Christian teachers talk about the importance of practicing spiritual disciplines, like fasting, Sabbath-keeping, and meditation. We have to be very careful when we talk about the benefits of such practices. It is all too easy to fall into a game of spiritual one-upmanship. When that happens, we end up with two classes of Christians in the church: a higher, spiritual elite, and a less highly regarded second class that cannot live up to the full rigors of the religion.

Christians have often fallen into this kind of perfectionism. For example, in the medieval church, it was a common assumption that professional religious people, meaning priests, monks, and nuns, were spiritually superior to the lay people who attended church. In striking a blow against this assumption, Protestants advocated the priesthood of all believers. It helps explain why Martin Luther loved this very letter of Paul.

A corollary of this two-class system that would have resulted from the Galatian churches adopting what the Judaizers were advocating is that males would have a superior position in the church, because only males could be circumcised.

If this is the way the Judaizers were arguing their case, then at stake were two conflicting visions of the church. Was the Christian church an egalitarian community, or was it a stratified, hierarchical community with various degrees of spiritual status? At the core of the community was there a central elite or were all Christians equal in status?

Again, this argument may sound familiar to us. There is always a tendency in Christian churches to create elites. Whether it be elitism grounded in spiritual disciplines or in ordination status or in mission outreach, we all too easily fall into traps of elevating one kind of Christian over others.

I myself experienced this as a child. In the churches my family attended there was a strong bias that if someone went into full-time Christian service, meaning the ordained ministry or the overseas mission field, then one was superior to those in the church who made their living in the secular world. There was constant pressure on young people to show the genuineness of their Christian commitment by opting for a vocation in full-time Christian service.

A DEBATE OVER WHAT CONSTITUTES THE BASIS OF CHRISTIAN MORALITY

Now there may also have been a third argument going on among some of these traveling evangelists, or possibly by a third Gentile party in the Galatian churches that disagreed with the traveling evangelists. In chapters 5 and 6 of his letter, Paul argues strongly that spiritual freedom does not mean license to do whatever we please.

This theme in the letter suggests that some of Paul's opponents were arguing that because Christ set Christians free, then Christians were exempt from morality. That would be especially true of the spiritual elite whose exalted status freed them from the common rules of morality that ordinary believers were expected to observe.

Or, advocates of this position may have been arguing that Christian freedom meant that *all* Christians, not just the spiritually elite, could just ignore ethics. If that were the case, then the Judaizers might have been arguing that the Mosaic law, especially its ethical commands, provided an important check against ethical libertinism. Christ sets us free, yes, but not to ignore the ethical dimensions of the life of faith.

But if Christianity has an ethic, where does it come from? Are ethics imposed from the outside, through laws and ethical strictures laid down by religious leaders and teachers? Or are ethics something that arise from within the inner spirit? If from the inner spirit, are all ethics then situational?

In response, Paul will argue that spiritual freedom is not just freedom *from* something, but also freedom *for* something. That something is the law of Christ, which Paul says is the law of love.

Once again, this may sound like a very familiar debate to us. We hear echoes of it in some of the ethical debates in Christian churches today. What is Christian freedom? Does it imply moral relativity? What does it really mean to live by the Holy Spirit?

So I think we can see that the Letter to the Galatians touches on issues and debates that have agitated Christians over and over again. No wonder this letter has had such a pervasive impact on Christian life and theology down through the ages.

2

Paul the Letter Writer
The Structure of the Letter to the Galatians

THOUGH THE CONTENT OF the Letter to the Galatians is theological, the theology comes to the Galatians in the format of a letter. It is, in fact, a real letter, not a fabricated one.

We are all familiar with the standard format of an American letter today. We usually start out a letter by placing a date and our sending location at the top of the page. We follow (especially in business letters) with the recipient's name, title, and address directly below.

We open the letter with a customary salutation (Dear So-and-So). Then follows the body of the letter, which can sometimes extend many pages. We close the letter with another customary phrase like, "sincerely yours," "cordially yours," "with warmest regards," or something similar. Then come the sender's signature and sometimes his or her printed name. Letter writers may depart from this format at times, but when they do, we recognize it as a departure from the standard format.

Letters written in the Greek and Roman worlds in Paul's day likewise followed a standard format, although it was a different format from ours. Paul uses that format in his own letters. It may help, therefore, to recognize that standard format as you read through his letters in the New Testament.

Where we open a letter with "Dear Addressee," a Greco-Roman letter opened with the sender's name. His or her name was the first word in the letter. Then came the addressee's name, followed by some greeting. Once again there was a standard greeting. In Greek it was *chairein*, which means *greetings* or *hello*.

Before the author launches into his or her main reason for writing, the author will usually add a word of thanksgiving for something as they recall the person to whom they are writing. Or the author may express hopes that the recipient is in good health.

After that comes the main body of the letter. At the end, the sender signs off with possibly some greetings from other people in his or her family or in the business. The last sentence or word of the letter will be some kind of closing salutation, like *good-bye*, or a closing wish for the recipient's health and welfare.

If you wish to see this format exhibited in a nutshell, just turn to the letter to Philemon in your New Testament. This is another of Paul's letters, written to an individual. As you read through it, you will find it keeps to the standard format precisely. As you read Paul's other letters in the New Testament, you will find they, too, usually follow this standard format, although sometimes the format has been obscured by editorial work on the letter after Paul's death.

The Letter to the Galatians follows this standard Greco-Roman letter format, with one notable exception. We will note it in the commentary when we come to it. But it may be helpful to you to recognize this format as you read through the letter.

There is one other characteristic feature to recognize about Paul's letters included in the New Testament. We find it in the Letter to the Galatians.

Often in his letters Paul will lay out an exposition of his theology in the first portion of the letter. After he has made his theological position clear, he will then turn to applying that theology to the behavior and daily life of Christians. Sometimes this is described as a turn from theology to ethics. But that is not always an accurate way to put it. Sometimes Paul is turning not only to what we might call ethics but to what today we would call spirituality. The point, however, is: of what practical significance is this theology? For Paul, theology always has practical significance.

You usually recognize this turning point in a Pauline letter by the appearance of the word *therefore*. It signals that Paul is turning from theological exposition to practical application.

The best example of this is to be found in Romans 12:1-2. In the first eleven chapters of Romans, Paul lays out his understanding of the gospel. It is the power of salvation to everyone who has faith. The unpacking of that conviction leads to some of the most influential theology ever written in the Christian church.

With verses 12:1-2, Paul turns to the practical application of that theology. He makes this turn with these words:

> I appeal to you therefore, brothers and sisters, by the mercies of God, to present your bodies as a living sacrifice, holy and acceptable to God, which is your spiritual worship. Do not be conformed to this world, but be transformed by the renewing of your minds, so that you may discern what is the will of God—what is good and acceptable and perfect.

Notice the prominence of that word *therefore* in the first sentence. It tells us that Paul is making this switch from exposition to application.

The word *therefore* will also signal an important redirection of the discussion in the Letter to the Galatians. So watch for it as you read your way through the letter.

3

A Weighty Greeting

GALATIANS 1:1-5

> [1] Paul an apostle—sent neither by human commission nor from human authorities, but through Jesus Christ and God the Father, who raised him from the dead— [2] and all the members of God's family who are with me,
>
> To the churches of Galatia:
>
> [3] Grace to you and peace from God our Father and the Lord Jesus Christ, [4] who gave himself for our sins to set us free from the present evil age, according to the will of our God and Father, [5] to whom be the glory forever and ever. Amen.

PAUL WRITES TO THE Galatians in the standard format of a Greco-Roman letter. So the letter opens with Paul's own name. He is the author of this letter. He is the one sending it. We are told that at the very start.

We are not told where Paul is writing from, but he is apparently writing from within a community of fellow Christian believers. He calls them "all the members of God's family who are with me." When we read Paul's letters, we do not get the sense that Paul worked as a lone-wolf missionary. He traveled and evangelized as a part of a team.

He names the recipients of the letter as "the churches of Galatia." Notice, it is churches in the plural. This letter is an authoritative message that Paul expects to be circulated among the churches in Galatia. We can believe that it was and that those churches studied it closely. The letter, after all, was preserved and later incorporated into what we now know as the New Testament.

When we read the word *churches*, we should be careful not to think of them as institutionalized religious organizations as we often think of churches today. They would not have had their own buildings that provided a visual identity marker in the surrounding community. They would not have had developed denominational bureaucracies as our larger denominations have today.

Instead, they would have been more informal gatherings of believers, closer to what many Christians today would consider small group ministries in our more established churches. They would have met in people's homes or possibly someone's shop. Some of the leaders might have been paid, but many of them would have worked on a volunteer basis.

The Greek word translated as *church* is the word *ekklesia*, from which we get the English word *ecclesiastical*. Although it has become customary in Christian circles to translate it as *church*, it is more properly translated as *assembly*. That puts the emphasis on the church as a gathering of people rather than as a brick-and-mortar building.

Lastly, Paul completes his opening with an expected salutation. He extends to the churches in Galatia his wish that they may receive grace and peace from God the Father and the Lord Jesus Christ. But it is not the standard salutation. The standard salutation in a Greco-Roman letter is the single word *chairein* (greetings).

Paul instead wishes the Galatians grace and peace. The word *grace* in Greek is *charis*. Its pronunciation would resonate with Gentile believers, because the standard Greek salutation *chairein* would have sounded very similar. But *charis* is a much richer word. It literally means *favor* or *goodwill,* either favor or goodwill felt for someone or shown to someone. It is the word Paul uses to describe the attitude of God toward us, especially God's goodwill extended to us in the life, death, and resurrection of Jesus.

The word *peace* (Greek: *eirene*), however, would have resonated with Jewish believers. It would have translated the more weighty Hebrew word *shalom.* In Greek, peace would have been most thought of as a cessation of conflict or an absence of war. That is the common association as well for the English word *peace.*

But the Hebrew word for peace (*shalom*) would have been much more expansive. It would certainly have embraced the cessation of conflict, but it would also have included the ideas of physical health and wholeness, economic prosperity, harmonious relationships between individuals and within society, and spiritual harmony with God. It stood for the total well-being of an individual, a society, and indeed of all creation. In many ways it was a synonym for salvation.

So when Paul is wishing grace and peace to the Galatians, he is extending a very rich blessing upon his recipients.

As we read these opening verses, however, we realize Paul is doing much more than writing a standard Greco-Roman letter opening. He expands upon the formula, and his expansions reveal both something of the tone of the letter and something of the content of its argument.

We notice, for example, that he opens the letter with more than just his name. He follows his name immediately with his office, that is, his calling as an apostle.

An apostle was a recognized office in the early church. It designated someone who was personally and authoritatively commissioned by God and sent to preach the gospel to others. Christians would expect their apostles to be someone who had spent time with Jesus during his earthly ministry—had heard Jesus teach, had watched Jesus perform his miracles, had witnessed the arrest and crucifixion of Jesus, and most importantly had an encounter with the risen Jesus. They were, therefore, eyewitnesses of the message about Jesus that they preached. This placed them in an authoritative position to verify the Christian message.

The Judaizing agitators who were troubling the Galatian churches seem to have been undermining Paul's authority and message by suggesting that Paul was either a secondary apostle or a phony apostle compared to the eleven original disciples of Jesus connected to the church in Jerusalem. Chief among those eleven original, surviving disciples was the apostle Peter.

Paul wants to discredit that aspersion against his apostleship right away as he opens his letter. So he follows his name with his office, his apostleship. He makes clear that his apostleship is not only legitimate but also equal to that of the Jerusalem disciples. He was not a secondary apostle because the leadership group in Jerusalem had so commissioned him. His commission came directly from Jesus Christ and God the Father.

Though Paul does not claim it here, we will find in other places in the New Testament (for example, 1 Cor 15:8), that he matches that supremely qualifying feature of an apostle, that is, a personal encounter with the risen Jesus. He is a witness to Jesus's resurrection through his Damascus Road experience. His call has come through the call of the God of the resurrection. The resurrection is the event that changes everything when we look at Jesus.

Paul also expands his salutation. We have noticed that he substitutes *grace* and *peace* for the standard Greco-Roman *greetings*. But he also expands upon that double wish, for he wishes these blessings as coming from God our Father and the Lord Jesus Christ.

By calling God our Father, Paul brings into our concept of God the thought of God's familial care. Like a loving father, God cares for his family, to which the Galatian believers belong. Whether Paul knew the wording of the Lord's Prayer or not, he certainly knew that Jesus's favorite way of addressing God was as *abba* (Aramaic for *daddy*). And we today cannot hear this description of God without immediately thinking of the opening words of Jesus's great prayer, "Our Father."

Notice, too, the designations that Paul gives to Jesus. He is the Lord Jesus Christ. Jesus is the name that Joseph and Mary gave him on his birth. It is a weighty name. Jesus is the Greek version of Joshua. And Joshua means *the Lord saves*.

But notice that the word Christ now seems to function as part of Jesus's personal name. *Christ* is the Greek translation for the Hebrew word *Messiah*. *Messiah* in Hebrew means God's anointed one. It functioned originally as a title or office (comparable to the similar use of *apostle* as a title). But by this early date in the history of the church (only some twenty-five years after Jesus's death), *Christ* has moved from a title to being part of the extended proper name of Jesus. It has continued as such through the last two thousand years of Christian history.

The word *Lord* (Greek: *kyrios*), however, is a title and has continued as such. It refers to Jesus's rulership, as the ruler who has been exalted to sit at the right hand of God and shares in God's authority and power, all this by means of Jesus's resurrection and ascension. Jesus is the master, in the many senses of that word. It is Paul's favorite word for referring to Jesus.

Jesus is the Lord Jesus Christ, "who gave himself for our sins to set us free from the present evil age, according to the will of our God and Father." Once again, Paul expands upon the name of Jesus by indicating the significance of Jesus not only through his titles, but also by what he has done.

As Paul looks at Jesus, he does not see Jesus primarily as a great spiritual teacher or as a guru. Paul does not, in fact, often refer to Jesus's teaching. Rather, for Paul Jesus is a savior or a liberator from oppression. Jesus does that primarily by his actions rather than his teaching.

This is why Paul speaks of Jesus as the one "who gave himself for our sins." For Paul, Jesus gave up his life voluntarily for the purpose of restoring harmony between human beings and God. Behind this concept lies the language of Jewish sacrifice. The Jewish sacrificial system had the purpose of restoring harmony between Israel and God after Israel's transgressions and betrayals. In a similar way, Jesus's death serves as an expiatory sacrifice that restores *shalom* with God. As the Letter to the Hebrews makes clear elsewhere in the New Testament, Jesus's death is the supreme and final sacrifice. It restores eternal harmony with God.

This sacrifice by and of Jesus "sets us free from the present evil age." The death of Jesus does more than restore harmony with God. It liberates us. Here Paul is turning to the language of Jewish eschatology, those teachings about how God would bring in his kingdom at the end of our present historical era.

Jewish eschatology involved a chronological dualism. On the one hand there is the present era of world existence. It is an era characterized by evil, corruption, and bondage. It is an era of disease and death; an era of psychological, social, political, and economic domination; an era when we can feel we are lost and exiled from our longed-for happiness; an era when we can feel as if God is absent and disengaged from our world. It is an era when we cannot feel or be truly free.

All that will change when the kingdom of God comes, when God sets all things right, destroying all the powers of oppression, and when the estrangement between God and us will be removed. When the kingdom of God comes, we will at last be able to feel and know that God is truly Emmanuel (God with us).

For Paul and for the whole of the New Testament, Jesus has brought that new era very close to us. It has arrived in Jesus's own death, resurrection, and ascension. Now Jesus is making his blessings available to us in advance through the gift of the Holy Spirit.

As Christians, therefore, we live in two eras simultaneously: in the old era of evil and corruption *and* in the new era of God's shalom and blessing. That is what makes the Christian life so exciting and so conflicting at the same time. We must constantly negotiate our lives in both eras at the same time.

This places enormous historical significance on Jesus's death, resurrection, and ascension. But Paul wants to make it clear, too, that behind all these events, it is God who has been at work. Everything happened by "the will of our God and Father."

The death of Jesus was not an accident. Nor was it something preventable if Jesus had just been a bit more diplomatic in his language or his actions. And it was not a normal martyr's death, where Jesus bore witness that God is great by dying out of his conviction.

No, the death of Jesus, and his subsequent resurrection and ascension, were willed by his Father, who through these actions was accomplishing his divine plan for the world. They were God's grace, his favor and goodwill, at work. No wonder Paul cannot help breaking out into a doxology at the close of the sentence. His theology issues in adoration, as I think all theology ultimately must.

There is one last thing to notice in these opening five verses of Galatians. Paul yokes Jesus Christ with God throughout. There is a kind of equality between God the Father and Jesus. The grace and peace we experience in our Christian lives comes from both. Now this is a rather astonishing way of talking for a Jewish monotheist, as Paul was raised to be. We see here some of the seeds of the later Christian doctrine of the Trinity.

So the first five verses of Galatians are short, but weighty indeed. This is what makes Paul such a dense writer at times. It seems that every word he uses comes with a weight of meaning and a richness of allusion. That's why Paul's letters, short as they are, provoke such long commentaries.

4

Give Me Your Attention

GALATIANS 1:6-10

> ^{6} I am astonished that you are so quickly deserting the one who called you in the grace of Christ and are turning to a different gospel— ^{7} not that there is another gospel, but there are some who are confusing you and want to pervert the gospel of Christ. ^{8} But even if we or an angel from heaven should proclaim to you a gospel contrary to what we proclaimed to you, let that one be accursed! ^{9} As we have said before, so now I repeat, if anyone proclaims to you a gospel contrary to what you received, let that one be accursed! ^{10} Am I now seeking human approval, or God's approval? Or am I trying to please people? If I were still pleasing people, I would not be a servant of Christ.

WE HAVE NOTICED HOW Paul's Letter to the Galatians begins in the recognizably standard format of a Greco-Roman letter, even if Paul expands upon that format. The congregations hearing this letter read aloud in their worship assemblies would have felt altogether at home.

But as the assembly leader read the next sentence, a shudder would have passed through the assembled listeners. The standard letter format called for Paul to express a word of thanksgiving for the people to whom he was writing or a prayer for their blessing and well-being. We see a beautiful example of this in the opening of Paul's Letter to the Philippians (Phil 1:3–11).

But there is no word of thanksgiving when Paul begins to address the Galatian believers. Instead his first words are, "I am astonished that you are so quickly deserting the one who called you in the grace of Christ." The Greek word that our translators have translated as *astonished* is the word *thaumazo*. It is an astonishment-rebuke word. It would have the same emotional feel as if an employer today were to say to a negligent employee, "I am just astonished at your careless inattention to detail. What were you thinking?"

Paul makes the feeling even worse when he begins to talk about their deserting God. Anyone familiar with the Old Testament, as some of the Galatians would have been, would recall the language of Exodus as it told the story of the Israelites at Sinai "deserting" God and turning to the worship of the Golden Calf (see Exod 32). For Paul, what is going on in the Galatian churches is a serious apostasy like that.

This language gives us an insight into Paul's sense of high alarm. The crisis in the Galatian churches is no tempest in a teapot, no high and mighty storm over nonessentials. It is instead a crisis that threatens a serious apostasy from the faith. It threatens the very essential message of the gospel. It is turning good news (the essential meaning of the word *gospel* in the Greek language) into bad news.

In chapter 3, Paul will ask the Galatians if someone has enchanted them. Has someone cast a magic spell on them? He cannot fathom any other reason why they have been duped by what in his eyes is a false understanding of the gospel. We might compare his attitude to that of a baffled parent today who has discovered that his or her child is dabbling in drugs. The crisis threatens the very life of these young church communities.

No doubt these words of Paul immediately seized the attention of his audience. They would have jumped in their seats and sat up straight. That would have been Paul's rhetorical purpose in writing as he has. He wants them to recognize that the debate going on in their churches is truly a crisis. If they give into the practices that the Judaizers are advocating, they will be compromising the gospel.

For Paul, the gospel is fundamentally a message about God's grace, God's gracious favor toward human beings. We can summarize that word of grace in this way: God is *for us*, not against us. Nowhere is that understanding of the gospel made clearer than in the letter that Paul was to write later to the church in Rome. Two quotations from Romans will make the point:

> But God proves his love for us in that while we still were sinners Christ died for us. (Rom 5:8)

> What then are we to say about these things? If God is for us, who is against us? He who did not withhold his own Son, but gave him up for all of us, will he not with him also give us everything else? (Rom 8:31–32)

The preaching and teaching of the Judaizers had obscured that fundamental word of grace. They had suggested that God is for us only if the Galatian believers also adopt a Jewish identity, by starting to observe Torah in their daily lives. This undoubtedly raised levels of confusion in the minds of the Galatian Gentile believers.

When Paul says that those Judaizing teachers are confusing them, the Greek word he uses is the verb *tarasso*. That verb suggests something more frightening than mental confusion. It might be better translated *terrifying* or *intimidating*. In their confusion, the Galatians may have been afraid that their salvation was in jeopardy. What could be more terrifying than that? Rather than their Christian faith bringing peace of mind, it was instead bringing high anxiety to these Galatians.

Paul wants to nip this terrifying message in the bud. So in verse 8 he proclaims a curse on anyone who might be preaching a gospel that is anything other than good news about God's gracious love for us. That curse rests even upon himself or any angel who might be found preaching such a so-called gospel. The Greek word translated as *cursed* is *anathema*. In the Greek translation of the Old Testament, this word was used to describe something that had been dedicated to God for destruction (See Lev 27:28–29 or Deut 7:26).

In verse 9, Paul repeats the word *anathema*. His double usage of the word indicates how strong his feelings are running. By using the strong word *anathema*, Paul is not practicing just rhetoric in his preaching. He is not flattering his listeners.

It was important to say because there is a suggestion in verse 10 that Paul's opponents were charging that Paul was preaching a cheap gospel, a gospel of God's grace that included no demands upon the lives of believers. According to those opponents, he was doing so to entice Gentiles into the faith by lowering the demands on their commitment.

But Paul retorts, "If I were still pleasing people, I would not be a servant of Christ." The word translated *servant* means literally *slave* in Greek. God's grace expressed in Christ does not free Paul or anyone else to follow their own whims. It calls them to service—service that is often hard and challenging and goes against the understanding of success pervasive in the surrounding culture.

5

A Genuine or Phony Apostle

GALATIANS 1:11-24

¹¹ For I want you to know, brothers and sisters, that the gospel that was proclaimed by me is not of human origin; ¹² for I did not receive it from a human source, nor was I taught it, but I received it through a revelation of Jesus Christ.

¹³ You have heard, no doubt, of my earlier life in Judaism. I was violently persecuting the church of God and was trying to destroy it. ¹⁴ I advanced in Judaism beyond many among my people of the same age, for I was far more zealous for the traditions of my ancestors. ¹⁵ But when God, who had set me apart before I was born and called me through his grace, was pleased ¹⁶ to reveal his Son to me, so that I might proclaim him among the Gentiles, I did not confer with any human being, ¹⁷ nor did I go up to Jerusalem to those who were already apostles before me, but I went away at once into Arabia, and afterwards I returned to Damascus.

¹⁸ Then after three years I did go up to Jerusalem to visit Cephas and stayed with him fifteen days; ¹⁹ but I did

not see any other apostle except James the Lord's brother.
[20] In what I am writing to you, before God, I do not
lie! [21] Then I went into the regions of Syria and Cilicia,
[22] and I was still unknown by sight to the churches of
Judea that are in Christ; [23] they only heard it said, "The
one who formerly was persecuting us is now proclaiming
the faith he once tried to destroy." [24] And they glorified
God because of me.

WITH VERSE 11, PAUL begins his defense of the gospel he preaches.
This defense will occupy the first part of the letter through chapter
4. He will return to it occasionally in chapters 5 and 6 as well.

In his defense of the gospel he is preaching, Paul will employ
a number of rhetorical arguments. We will note each one as we
come to it. With verse 11, he will start to employ his first argument, an argument based upon his own life. He will tell something
of his own story.

In the process he will also answer a charge that his opponents
were probably spreading through the Galatian churches. They may
have been arguing that Paul was actually a phony apostle. They
may have been saying that Paul had not been a member of Jesus's
circle of disciples during Jesus's earthly ministry, nor had he been
a witness of Jesus's resurrection during those forty days before Jesus's final ascension.

Or they may have been arguing that Paul was a secondary
apostle, not of the same spiritual stature as those twelve original
disciples who constituted the core of the church in Jerusalem. In
fact, they would have argued, those original apostles had commissioned Paul to be an apostle. His understanding of the gospel,
therefore, would be subject to their authoritative interpretation.

So in defending his understanding of the gospel, Paul was
also defending his office as a genuine apostle of Jesus Christ.

Before we launch into his defense, we should note, however,
how Paul softens the impact of the dramatic rebuke he expressed
in opening his letter in verses 6–10. There he had wanted to grab
the Galatians' attention by his very strong language that would
have made, as I said earlier, his audience shudder.

By his use of strong language, he ran the risk of shutting down their minds and hardening their hearts. So before he proceeds further, he addresses them as brothers and sisters. His language is intended to appeal to the familial relationship he has with them. He may feel alarm over their welfare, but he still feels deep affection for them. He is not writing this letter to alienate them, but to warn them of the serious theological issues involved in the debate going on in their churches.

In defense of the gospel he preaches, Paul says that it is a gospel he received through a direct revelation of Jesus Christ. Other leaders in the church had not instructed him in the gospel he preaches. Nor had he received it by a process of instruction from a church community in preparation for baptism, as would have been true for most new converts. Instead, he received the gospel through a revelation of Jesus Christ.

Read his language carefully. He does not say he was instructed by Christ, as if Christ directly dictated the gospel to Paul. That is how Muslims understand that Muhammad received the Koran. The angel Gabriel dictated the Koran to Muhammad who committed its words to memory.

That kind of revelation is not what Paul has in mind. He says he received his gospel "through a revelation of Jesus Christ." Paul seems to be referring to his encounter with Jesus in the vision he has on the Damascus Road, which is recounted in Acts 9:1–9.

That vision turns not only Paul's life upside down, but also his theology. He is confronted with the basic Christian conviction that Jesus is Lord. Jesus is alive and he resides in heaven at the right hand of God. There is also an unexpected unity between Jesus and the Christians whom Paul is persecuting. In persecuting Christians, Paul is in fact persecuting Jesus.

This vision completely upends all that Paul had previously believed.[1] He claims it is the source of his gospel.

Now, I have no doubt that Paul spent a great deal of time and energy reflecting on this vision and its implications after the fact.

1. For more on how this vision experience transforms Paul and his theology, see the theological reflection which follows on page 31.

That may be one thing he was doing during his stay in Arabia that he mentions in verse 17. And undoubtedly that time of reflection involved some deep reflection on the Old Testament as well. All that time of reflection may have been the way in which Paul unpacked the logic of his vision of Jesus and its implications for his life work. In that respect, they were part of the revelation of Jesus through which he receives his gospel.

But it all begins with that one, decisive, and seminal experience of Jesus on the Damascus Road. By laying claim to this experience as the source of his gospel, Paul is also claiming his genuineness as well as his independence as an apostle of Jesus Christ.

In verses 11–17, we glimpse something of the dramatic transformation that occurred within Paul once he had that vision of Jesus on the Damascus Road. In these verses he describes himself as a zealous and exemplary Jew. He adhered to the theological party of the Pharisees, who advocated not only a strict observance of Torah, but also its application to every aspect of daily life. Their purpose was to erase the separation of the sacred and secular spheres of life, to make all of daily life holy.

Before his conversion, Paul saw the Christian movement as compromising the theological integrity of Judaism by seemingly placing Jesus as superior to Torah. That was a horror to Paul, in part because, to Paul, Jesus was not only a failed or fake Messiah, Jesus was, as a result of his crucifixion, a Messiah cursed by God. The Christian movement also threatened to soften the rigid dividing line between Jews as God's people and Gentiles as those outside.

After his encounter with Jesus in the vision, Paul began to preach a theological position that is exactly the opposite to the Pharisee position he had formerly espoused. Furthermore, he will become convinced that God has chosen him for a mission of bringing the gospel to the Gentiles.

The language Paul uses to describe this call in verses 15–16 recalls the call of the Old Testament prophets, especially the call of Jeremiah. Note how closely Paul's language resonates with the words of God when God calls Jeremiah to be a prophet:

> Before I formed you in the womb I knew you, and before you were born I consecrated you; I appointed you a prophet to the nations. (Jer 1:5)

Paul sees his call to be an apostle to the Gentiles as part of a larger plan of God. The significance of his life is to be found in that larger plan and the work that God has set him aside to do in that larger plan. God has chosen him to extend God's redemptive work in Jesus Christ to the peoples who lie outside of Israel.

Paul once again emphasizes his independence from the leadership group in Jerusalem by telling us that after this encounter with Jesus, he did not immediately hasten to Jerusalem to have his call blessed by the apostles residing there. Instead, he retreats to Arabia for a time. By Arabia he may be referring to the area of the Negev, south of the Dead Sea or the Sinai desert. We cannot be sure.

What was he doing during this time in Arabia? Some scholars have suggested that Paul was seeking to fulfill his call to evangelize the Gentiles by immediately going and preaching the gospel to those living in the desert regions south of Judea. Others have suggested Paul spent his time in the desert reflecting upon his experience with Jesus and thinking through its many implications. Maybe he was doing both. We cannot be sure.

After that time he returned to Damascus, where he undoubtedly became engaged with the Christian community residing there, proclaiming the faith he had tried to destroy. This must have surprised and shocked not only that Christian community, but also his former colleagues in the Pharisee party.

Only after three years of his life as a Christian does Paul finally make a visit to Jerusalem. There he spends fifteen days with the apostle Peter.[2] I am sure they talked about many things. Paul may have shared his experience with Jesus and his call to evangelize the nations. Peter may have shared stories about the earthly

---

2. Peter's name in Aramaic was Cephas.

ministry of Jesus and the events of his crucifixion, resurrection, and ascension.

During this time, Paul also had a brief encounter with James, the brother of Jesus, who was emerging as the chief leader of the church in Jerusalem.

Paul may have seen his commission to be an apostle as independent from the apostolic circle in Jerusalem, but he also did not see his ministry as set in opposition to the church in Jerusalem. Their ministries may be distinct, but they are to work in partnership, not in opposition. Therefore, harmony with the Jerusalem church leaders was important to Paul.

6

Theological Reflection
Paul's Conversion and Missionary Vision

THE CONVERSION OF PAUL is one of the most momentous events in the two-thousand-year history of Christianity. Its impact can be compared to a gigantic meteorite that crashes into the sea and sends shock wave after shock wave racing across the ocean and beating against every shore.

Paul's encounter with Jesus in the vision he has on the Damascus Road is described three times in the book of Acts. The first account comes in Acts 9:1–9. It is told in a third-person narrative. The second and third accounts come in Acts 22:4–16 and Acts 26:9–18. In both of these accounts, Paul personally describes the experience.

Another account of his conversion is told in Galatians 1:13–17. It is much briefer and rather allusive in its details. From the Galatians account, however, we get some additional details that help us understand the Acts accounts.

The encounter with Jesus on Damascus Road is not only central to the life and ministry of Paul, but it is central, too, to understanding Paul's theological position in the Letter to the Galatians. And I think it speaks powerfully to the theological challenge faced by Christians today in our evangelism. For that reason, I want to pause a moment and look at this momentous event and its implications.

THE CHARACTER OF PAUL'S CONVERSION

The first thing to say about Paul's[1] conversion is that it is not exactly a conversion, if you are thinking of conversion in the way the Protestant reformers or the American revivalist movement tend to use the term. The literal meaning of *conversion* is a turning around, a kind of 180-degree turn in one's way of living or in one's way of thinking or both. In that sense, Paul's experience is truly a conversion. It involves a dramatic turn around in his life.

But Paul's conversion does not fit the typical pattern of a release from a sense of sin, guilt, and despair, and a gift of forgiveness, peace, and harmony with God. None of the accounts we read of Paul's vision give any sense that as he was walking that road to Damascus, he was deeply troubled within by doubts, guilt, and a troubled conscience. He is no Martin Luther seeking to know a gracious God.

To get a sense of what his conversion meant to Paul, we need to read the conversion accounts in Acts and Galatians in the light of what Paul says in Philippians 3:4–6:

> If anyone else has reason to be confident in the flesh, I have more: circumcised on the eighth day, a member of the people of Israel, of the tribe of Benjamin, a Hebrew born of Hebrews; as to the law, a Pharisee; as to zeal, a persecutor of the church; as to righteousness under the law, blameless.

This passage gives us a sense of how Paul saw himself as a Jew before his encounter with Jesus. He saw himself as an exemplary Jew. He came from good Jewish stock. He lived strictly by

1. I am using throughout my discussion Paul's Christian name of Paul. Before his conversion his Jewish name was Saul. In the accounts of his conversion, he is referred to or addressed as Saul. As he later settled into his Christian life and vocation, Saul substituted his name for the more Gentile Paul.

the Torah. He was zealous in his commitment to the God of Israel and in defense of God's cause. He was, in fact, blameless in how he lived by the strictures of righteousness laid down by the Torah.

We get no sense of a troubled conscience in any of this language, nor in the sketchy language we find in Galatians 1:13–14. When Paul becomes a Christian, it is not because he becomes convinced that there is something inherently evil or sinful about the life he was living as a Jew.

But a transformation does occur. We need to turn again to the Philippians passage to get a sense of what this transformation was. Hear what Paul says in the three verses that immediately follow the verses I quoted above:

> Yet whatever gains I had, these I have come to regard as loss because of Christ. More than that, I regard everything as loss because of the surpassing value of knowing Christ Jesus my Lord. For his sake I have suffered the loss of all things, and I regard them as rubbish, in order that I may gain Christ and be found in him, not having a righteousness of my own that comes from the law, but one that comes through faith in Christ, the righteousness from God based on faith. (Phil 3:7–9)

The transformation in Paul is a transformation of his consciousness, of his way of thinking and his way of valuation. He sees and feels in dramatically new ways than he did when he was a Pharisee. That will make a 180-degree difference in how he thinks and how he lives.

NOTICING THE DETAILS OF PAUL'S CONVERSION ACCOUNTS

I think we can be more precise about what this transformation in consciousness involved. Let's start by looking at the account of Paul's encounter with Jesus recounted in Acts 9:1–9.

> Meanwhile Saul, still breathing threats and murder against the disciples of the Lord, went to the high priest

and asked him for letters to the synagogues at Damascus, so that if he found any who belonged to the Way, men or women, he might bring them bound to Jerusalem.

Now as he was going along and approaching Damascus, suddenly a light from heaven flashed around him. He fell to the ground and heard a voice saying to him, "Saul, Saul, why do you persecute me?" He asked, "Who are you, Lord?" The reply came, "I am Jesus, whom you are persecuting. But get up and enter the city, and you will be told what you are to do." The men who were traveling with him stood speechless because they heard the voice but saw no one. Saul got up from the ground, and though his eyes were open, he could see nothing; so they led him by the hand and brought him into Damascus. For three days he was without sight, and neither ate nor drank.

First of all in the experience after the flash of heavenly light, Paul hears a voice speaking to him; "Saul, Saul, why do you persecute me?" Paul must have understood this voice immediately as a divine voice, but why would this divine voice charge him with persecuting him? This must have shocked and confused Paul. So he asks, "Who are you, Lord?"

Notice that Paul addresses the voice by the divine title/name *Lord*. The response he receives must have come like a lightning bolt to the very center of his soul. "I am Jesus, whom you are persecuting." The divine voice coming from heaven is the voice of Jesus.

How can this be? Paul must have thought. For Paul the Pharisee, Jesus was a failed or false Messiah. And most importantly, he was a cursed Messiah.

This takes some unpacking to understand. It involves the way Deuteronomy 21:22–23 was being read in Paul's day. These two verses specify that the body of a person executed by hanging was not to be left hanging overnight. It was to be buried immediately. Why? Because "anyone hung on a tree is under God's curse."

Jewish interpreters in Paul's day understood that this verse applied to anyone who was crucified. A crucified man was cursed by God. We know from what Paul will later say in Galatians 3:13

that Paul read the Deuteronomy verse in this way. So Paul the Pharisee would have regarded Jesus as a man cursed by God by the very fact that Jesus had been executed by crucifixion.

Now, Paul encounters this same Jesus as not only alive, but also exalted into heaven. Jesus speaks with the voice of divinity. In addressing Jesus as Lord, Paul even addresses Jesus by the proper title/name of God in the Greek translation of the Old Testament.

Furthermore, this Jesus tells Paul that he is persecuting him. How can that be? Paul would have regarded Jesus as dead. How can you persecute a dead man? But Paul *is* persecuting the Christian community. In the vision, Paul comes to understand that there is such a close and intimate union between Jesus and his community that to persecute the community is, in fact, to persecute Jesus. We may find here the very seed of Paul's later conviction that the community of faith is indeed the body of Christ.

TURNING PAUL'S CONSCIOUSNESS UPSIDE DOWN

The effect of these revelations must have been truly soul shaking, a spiritual earthquake in Paul's consciousness. Paul begins to see God and God's work in the world in a dramatically different way than he did as a Pharisee. He will value his Jewish past in a totally different way. When we return to the Philippians passage, we find him saying that, as a result of his encounter with Jesus, he sees that all in his Jewish past that he was so confident and proud about is pure rubbish.

What Paul says in that Philippians passage reminds me of a similar experience that involved a dramatic change of consciousness in the mind and feelings of an outstanding Christian saint and theologian, Thomas Aquinas. Aquinas can stand in spiritual stature with men like Paul, Augustine of Hippo, Jean Calvin, and Karl Barth. His writings were voluminous and of such depth that they are foundational for much of the theological tradition of Roman Catholicism today.

One of his companions reports that toward the end of Aquinas' life, Thomas heard Jesus speak to him during mass, saying,

"You have written well of me, Thomas? What reward would you have for your labor?" Thomas replied, "Nothing but you, Lord."

He seems afterward to have experienced some kind of spiritual vision or ecstasy. Aquinas never shared precisely the details of what he experienced. But it dramatically changed the course of his work. He stopped writing and never wrote again during the remaining months of his life. When his confessor urged him to take up his writing, he responded, "Reginald, I can do no more. Such secrets have been revealed to me that all I have written now appears to be of little value."[2]

Aquinas, like Paul, had apparently experienced Jesus in such a dramatically profound way that it completely transformed his consciousness and behavior. Aquinas was known as the "angelic doctor" because of the sweetness of his disposition. What he had experienced, therefore, cannot be understood as a conversion experience in the pattern of Martin Luther. It must be understood in the pattern of Paul's Damascus encounter with Jesus.

PAUL'S CALL TO EVANGELIZE THE GENTILES

Now, in Galatians 1:13–17, Paul seems to be saying that his encounter with Jesus also involved his commissioning as an apostle to evangelize the Gentiles. When we read the account given in Acts 9, we find no words to that effect. But in the other two Acts accounts, which Paul recites himself, he does indicate that his experience involved some kind of call to preach to the Gentiles. In Acts 22:14–15, that call comes through the voice of Ananias, who baptized Paul. In Acts 26:16–18, the call comes directly from Jesus during the Damascus Road vision.

It is impossible, therefore, to determine with precision just how the call came to Paul. Maybe an awareness of the call evolved as Paul reflected on his experience during the time he spent in Arabia. We cannot know. But it is clear from Galatians that the call

2. An account of Thomas' experience can be found in numerous biographies of the man. I have relied primarily on the entry on Saint Thomas Aquinas in Herbermann et al., *Catholic Encyclopedia*.

was associated in his mind with his encounter with Jesus on the Damascus Road.

That call, too, must have been part of the soul shaking that his encounter with Jesus involved. As a Pharisee, Paul would have taken a very narrow view of who constituted the people of God. It was the Israelites, that religious-ethnic group of Jews who traced their lineage back to Abraham and who lived by the Torah that God had given them through Moses. Gentiles could only share in the privilege of belonging to that people by converting to Judaism.

But now as a result of his encounter with Jesus, the cursed and rejected Messiah, Paul saw how God was opening up membership in his people to Gentiles as Gentiles, not as Jews. Jesus was not just the Jewish Messiah. He was Savior of the world. This realization would have involved a dramatic transformation of Paul's consciousness.

One consequence of that change in consciousness is the Letter to the Galatians and its key conviction that "if you belong to Christ, then you are Abraham's offspring, heirs to the promise" (Gal 3:29).

At the heart of his gospel is the good news that the outsider can become an insider in the circle of the people of God. God is not deliberately choosing some people for the privilege of belonging to his family and excluding others. God's grace extends to all people, for God is *for* his whole creation. He calls all people to respond to his grace by living in grateful trust in his love as expressed for us in Jesus Christ.

A WORD OF CAUTION TO CHRISTIANS TODAY

I find in all this a caution to Christians today. Let us not be too hasty in deciding who is in the circle of God's love and who is not. The boundaries may be much more porous and blurry than we feel they should be. So Paul found.

Through his encounter with Jesus, Paul came to understand that God was far more inclusive than Paul the Pharisee believed. God was calling Gentiles to belong to his family and not just Jews alone. And God called Gentiles as Gentiles, not as Jewish converts. This had already been mirrored in Jesus's ministry as he called sinners, tax collectors, harlots, and other outsiders to enter into his Kingdom.

Unfortunately, many Americans do not see this God and this Jesus reflected in the life and message of the Christian churches they find around them. Far too many people today regard Christian churches not as inclusive, but as judgmental, discriminatory, and excluding. Many Christian communities are so because they feel they are called "to be separated" from the world and its evil ways. We must be holy as God is holy. That means no compromise with the ways of the world.

By nature, I like life to be black or white, not grey. But I am not sure we can draw firm boundaries around the community of faith without doing injustice to the gospel, for I am convinced that God is far more inclusive in his call than we Christians are. We need to take heed to the parable that Jesus tells of the farmer's field planted with both wheat and weeds (Matt 13:24–30, 36–43). We must be patient in letting God sort out the distinctions lest we destroy some of the good wheat by our premature judgments.

This message comes sharply home for me in our world today of religious pluralism. I am a firm Christian believer. I believe Jesus Christ is Savior of the world. But I think Christians need to be very, very cautious in their judgments on adherents of other religious traditions. Will they be saved when the last judgment comes or not?

I believe we simply do not know. The God who surprised Paul by showing grace to Gentiles as Gentiles, not as converts to Judaism, may surprise us as well by showing grace to adherents of other religions, not as Christian converts.

This is not to assert universal salvation. The New Testament indicates there is a real risk in refusing the grace of God. But we need to be cautious in trying to define precisely what faith or refusal may look like in God's perspective. Our task is not to sort out the saved from the unsaved. Our task is the same as Paul's: to faithfully preach the gospel in word and in deed.

7

A Fateful Agreement

GALATIANS 2:1-10[1]

[1] Then after fourteen years I went up again to Jerusalem with Barnabas, taking Titus along with me. [2] I went up in response to a revelation. Then I laid before them (though only in a private meeting with the acknowledged leaders) the gospel that I proclaim among the Gentiles, in order to make sure that I was not running, or had not run, in vain. [3] But even Titus, who was with me, was not compelled to be circumcised, though he was a Greek. [4] But because of false believers secretly brought in, who slipped in to spy on the freedom we have in Christ Jesus, so that they might enslave us— [5] we did not submit to them even for a moment, so that the truth of the gospel might always remain with you. [6] And from those who were supposed to be acknowledged leaders (what they

---

1. When Paul wrote his letter, he did not add chapter and verse numeration to the text. That numeration was added several hundred years after the letter was composed. I use the chapter and verse references for the purposes of keeping our place as we work through the text. But Paul would not have had them in mind when he was composing his thoughts.

actually were makes no difference to me; God shows no partiality)—those leaders contributed nothing to me. [7] On the contrary, when they saw that I had been entrusted with the gospel for the uncircumcised, just as Peter had been entrusted with the gospel for the circumcised [8] (for he who worked through Peter making him an apostle to the circumcised also worked through me in sending me to the Gentiles), [9] and when James and Cephas and John, who were acknowledged pillars, recognized the grace that had been given to me, they gave to Barnabas and me the right hand of fellowship, agreeing that we should go to the Gentiles and they to the circumcised.

[10] They asked only one thing, that we remember the poor, which was actually what I was eager to do.

WITH THE BEGINNING OF chapter 2, Paul continues his defense of the gospel he preaches and of his apostleship. He recounts the essential facts of his second visit to Jerusalem. It was a far more momentous visit than his first visit recounted in 1:18–24. In that first visit he met informally with Peter. It was probably a time when two emerging leaders of the church had an opportunity to get to know each other personally and engage in some one-on-one conversation.

This second visit had the character of two official parties of two separate churches (Jerusalem and Antioch) meeting for consultation on a matter of theological dispute. It resulted in an agreement that has shaped the character of Christianity ever since.

This second visit comes fourteen years after Paul's first, informal visit with Peter. In the intervening years, Paul had returned to his own native region of Cilicia, a region in the southeastern corner of modern day Turkey. We do not know anything about Paul's doings in these years. He undoubtedly spent many hours reflecting on his encounter with the risen Jesus as well as preaching the gospel to the residents of this largely Gentile region. At some point he moved to Antioch. He became a part of a very active and growing church.

Along with Rome and Alexandria in Egypt, Antioch was a great metropolis in the Greco-Roman world. It was a Greek-founded and largely Greek-speaking city that dominated the eastern shore of the Mediterranean. It was an economic power. It disseminated Greek culture in the eastern Mediterranean. It was the seat of Roman rule over Syria and Palestine.

A Christian community had started up in Antioch shortly after Christian missionaries began to spread out from the mother church in Jerusalem. According to Acts 11:26, followers of Jesus were first called Christians in Antioch.

The church that sprang up in Antioch drew both Jewish and Gentile adherents. While in Judea and Galilee, Gentile adherents to Christianity were no longer an oddity, they were still a minority within the Christian movement. But in Antioch, the Gentile contingent was substantial.

As a result, the church in Antioch posed a challenge for the new Christian movement, a challenge it had not been forced to confront before. What was the relationship between traditional Judaism and this new Christian movement? Was Christianity just a subset of Judaism or was it something that was bursting out of its generation within Judaism?

One is reminded of the words of Jesus about trying to pour new wine into old wineskins. Could the new wine of the Christian movement be contained in the old wineskin of traditional Judaism, or was this new wine bursting out of that skin? (See Mark 2:22).

Jesus had warned that the danger of trying to pour new wine into old wineskins was that both the new wine and the old skin might be lost. Was that indeed happening in Antioch and in all the other churches where Gentiles were becoming a significant component of the congregation's membership?

This confusion came to a crisis, it seems, in the Antioch church. And so the Antioch church commissioned Paul and his colleague Barnabas to travel to Jerusalem and work out an answer to the question with the apostolic leaders of the Jerusalem church.

The choice of Barnabas was probably deliberate. He had become a Christian in the Jerusalem church, but he also traveled with Paul in his first missionary endeavor into Asia Minor. He could be an important bridge figure between Jewish Christianity and Gentile Christianity. They chose to take along with them another member of Paul's evangelistic team, a Gentile Christian named Titus.

The consultation was fraught with danger. Sensitivities on both sides were probably high. We get the sense that Paul himself was on edge. Throughout this passage, he makes a point of his independence from the Jerusalem authorities as he did in the previous passage in chapter 1. He keeps referring to the apostolic leaders in Jerusalem as the supposedly acknowledged leaders. He knows they are the leaders that run the Jerusalem church, but he seems to be hesitant to acknowledge them officially.

He also says that the visit to Jerusalem was not due to the Jerusalem leaders summoning him to give an account of his missionary endeavors. The visit, he says, was motivated by a revelation from God. God is a player in this consultation. He also calls his most vocal opponents "false believers."

Yet, Paul seems to be concerned that the Jerusalem authorities will disown him and deny the legitimacy of his evangelistic work. He wants those powers to acknowledge him.

This could be a sign that Paul harbors some doubts about the direction he is pursuing and he needs the Jerusalem apostles to help put those doubts to rest. But probably not. As we read Paul in this letter and others, he comes across as supremely confident in the direction he is taking. But we get a sense in all Paul's letters that he is constantly concerned about maintaining the unity of the Christian movement. He does not want the work he is doing to create a schism in the church, leading to two separate expressions of Christianity that are suspicious of each other.

The book of Acts also describes this crisis that arose in Antioch. It records two visits of Paul to Jerusalem. In one, Barnabas and Paul bring financial relief to the impoverished Jerusalem church (Acts 11:27–30). In the other visit, Paul and Barnabas come to Jerusalem for an official consultation, the goal of which is to resolve the basis on which Gentile Christians are incorporated into the church (recounted in Acts 15:1–29).

Scholars have spilled much ink trying to harmonize what Acts says with what Paul says in this portion of Galatians. Is Paul describing something that happened on that first visit, or is he recounting his memories of what happened at the official consultation that constituted the second visit?

If you are writing a history of early Christianity, the issue is an important one, for what you decide affects your understanding not only of how the conflict evolved but also of how Paul's career developed. But an answer to the question is not essential for an understanding of Paul's rhetoric in the Letter to the Galatians. So I propose to ignore the historical question and focus entirely on unpacking his rhetorical argument.

The flash point in the controversy centered upon the issue of circumcision. Circumcision was one of the essential identity markers of Judaism in this era as it has been throughout all eras of Jewish history. It defined who was a Jew and who was not (that is, if you were male in gender).

Circumcision denoted who belonged to the covenant community of God and who did not. (It compares in importance to the significance that many Christians give to the question of whether a person is born again or not. Being born again identifies the true Christian, in their eyes.)

This belief was grounded in one of the stories told of Abraham in Genesis 17. There, God makes a covenant with Abraham, promising to make of Abraham's descendants a multitude of nations. Abraham and his descendants indicate their adherence to this covenant by the practice of circumcision, a practice instituted by God himself. In Genesis 17:14 comes this fateful sentence: "Any uncircumcised male who is not circumcised in the flesh of his foreskin shall be cut off from his people; he has broken my covenant."

The importance of circumcision as an identity marker of Judaism was reinforced in the second century BC during the Maccabean revolt. That revolt erupted in response to a Greek effort to force Jews to give up their ancestral ways and conform to Greek culture. It had involved an attempt to stamp out circumcision among Jews.

So if the new Christian movement was to pour its new wine into the old wineskin of Judaism, then it was going to be necessary for Gentile Christians to live by the Torah, including the demand for circumcision.

Paul opposed this demand. He helped bring the issue to a head in Jerusalem by bringing Titus along as a part of his and Barnabas' delegation. But significantly for Paul, the Jerusalem church authorities did not compel Titus to be circumcised.

Although the language Paul uses in 2:1–10 is often fragmented and conveys a strong hint of his hyper suspicions, he does record the agreement that the apostolic authorities in Jerusalem worked out with the delegation from Antioch. Those apostolic authorities included two original disciples of Jesus, Peter and John (the son of Zebedee), as well as James (the brother of Jesus who was becoming the dominant leader of the Jerusalem church).

First, the Jerusalem authorities acknowledge Paul's legitimate calling as an apostle, especially as an apostle to the Gentiles. Peter, on the other hand, is acknowledged as the apostle to the Jewish community. Circumcision would not be required of Gentile male converts.

Second, the agreement meant that the two communities of Christians, the Jewish community and the Gentile community, would live in mutual recognition of each other, even if they did not fully follow a common way of life. There was agreement on essentials, but disagreement on nonessentials. Paul's concern to maintain the unity of the church had been achieved.

In verse 10, however, Paul mentions one request the Jerusalem church places upon Paul's Gentile converts. They ask those converts to remember the Jerusalem church financially. This is something Paul will be very solicitous to do through his evangelistic journeys. In several letters he refers to the collection he takes up on behalf of the Jerusalem church. It is a major theme of 2 Corinthians 8–9, where Paul says, "God loves a cheerful giver."

Paul never flinches from the task of fund-raising. He pursues it with vigor.

8

The Agreement Falls Apart

GALATIANS 2:11–14

> [11] But when Cephas came to Antioch, I opposed him to his face, because he stood self-condemned; [12] for until certain people came from James, he used to eat with the Gentiles. But after they came, he drew back and kept himself separate for fear of the circumcision faction. [13] And the other Jews joined him in this hypocrisy, so that even Barnabas was led astray by their hypocrisy. [14] But when I saw that they were not acting consistently with the truth of the gospel, I said to Cephas before them all, "If you, though a Jew, live like a Gentile and not like a Jew, how can you compel the Gentiles to live like Jews?"

IF PAUL THOUGHT THE consultation in Jerusalem (which he describes in verses 1–10) had settled the matter on what basis Jewish and Gentile Christians joined in church life, he was to be bitterly disappointed.

Many church disputes do not simply dissolve away once an official church council adjudicates a dispute and makes a definitive decision. The parties in the dispute may continue to wrangle for years or decades before the issue finally settles down one way or the other. A good example is the theological dispute over Arianism in the fourth century. Despite the official pronouncement of the Council of Nicaea in AD 325, the controversy continued to roil church life for nearly a century to come.

Another good example is the debate over the legitimacy of ordaining women, a controversy of our own day. Though many Protestant denominations like my own have affirmed that legitimacy through official pronouncements from their church councils, many Protestants still contest the issue as do the Roman Catholic and Orthodox churches.

Official pronouncements do not silence debate. That seems to have been the case in the dispute over whether Gentile Christians had to become Jewish in order to be genuine Christians. Paul was to discover this personally in his home church of Antioch. There, the decision of the Jerusalem consultation seems to have been put into practice. Even the apostle Peter (Cephas) abided by the decision and freely participated in meals with Gentile Christians.

Jews and Gentiles sharing in meals together was another big issue that separated Jews from Gentiles. Jews had special dietary laws that governed what kinds of foods were clean or kosher to eat and which were not. But in addition, sharing a meal in the ancient world implied that the participants accepted each other. Jews were well known in the ancient Greco-Roman world for not sharing meals with Gentiles. It was another of the Jewish identity markers.

The Antioch church seemed to ignore this restriction until a group of people came from the Jerusalem church and called in question what the Antioch church was doing. We do not know if they were official delegates from the apostle James, head of the Jerusalem church. If they were, they would indicate that James had changed his mind from the agreement he signed at the Jerusalem consultation. On the other hand, they may have not had any official commission from James. They would, therefore, have falsely claimed to represent the viewpoint of James.

On whatever basis they arrived in Antioch, they put the Antioch church into turmoil. Soon, the Jewish members of the church were withdrawing from participation in meals with Gentile members. This may have been a withdrawal from all meals, or just a withdrawal from the Lord's Supper. We don't know for sure. But the withdrawal severed fellowship between the two branches of the church.

Surprisingly, Peter also participated in this withdrawal, although he had been eating with Gentiles before these people from Jerusalem arrived. We wonder why. Was Peter having second thoughts about the decision made in the Jerusalem consultation? Did these representatives from Jerusalem, who seemed to have the approval of James, intimidate Peter? Was Peter compromising for the sake of church peace? Or was Peter trying to save the Jewish Christian community from attack by Jewish zealots?

We do not know Peter's motives. That gives us some idea of how messy and hazy the dynamics of the Antioch church must have been.

Paul stands nearly alone in upholding the decision of the Jerusalem consultation. Even his close colleague Barnabas goes to the other side. This defection by Barnabas must have been a great disappointment to Paul. Acts 15 tells us that Paul and Barnabas were to split up their partnership in missionary endeavors. This separation may partly be fallout from Barnabas' defection in this theological dispute. We do not know, but we can see how the theological dispute created tremendous tension among church leaders and friends.

Why was Paul so alarmed by Peter's and Barnabas' actions? Here it may be helpful to see the actions in our own contemporary terms. The Jewish insistence on separation in meals between Jewish and Gentile Christians threatened to create a kind of spiritual segregation in the Christian movement. Jews and Gentiles would both be Christian, but they would practice their faith in rigidly separated communities.

As we have learned from the American experience with racial separation, "separate but equal" inevitably means that one community is considered inferior to the other. If the separation in meals had continued, Christianity would likely have split into two separate communities that would have come to be at odds with each other.

Paul saw Christ as dissolving this wall of separation between Jew and Gentile. That was part of the good news of the gospel. But if the policy of separate meals between the two communities became established practice, then this spiritual segregation would become not only established policy, but also, ultimately, established doctrine. And Christ would have died in vain.

Paul, therefore, felt compelled to fight the practice with all the passion he had. For him, the integrity of the gospel was indeed at stake. So Paul has the courage to directly challenge Peter, chief of the apostles, and accuse him of hypocrisy. This happened in front of the whole church. The tension level in that particular church gathering must have soared into the emotional stratosphere.

We do not know how the situation in Antioch resolved itself. Some scholars believe the conservative Jewish Christians from Jerusalem won the day. Paul then had to leave the Antioch church and take up an independent ministry. Others think Paul won the day. If he did, then we can understand why he is so alarmed when this same controversy pops up in the churches he had founded in Galatia. Once again, he has to fight a battle that he may have thought he won already.

In all this we can begin to see how life in the early church was not always calm and peaceful. Theological principles as well as church practices were being debated, raising intense passions. How the Christian movement decided would have lasting consequences for Christianity.

In my own denomination (the Presbyterian Church, U.S.A.), when a person is ordained a minister or an elder, he or she is asked to take an oath of ordination. A number of questions form this oath. One is: Do you promise to further the peace, unity, and purity of the church? We promise to further all three together.

But if you think about it, this is a promise that is nearly impossible to keep. It is easy to obtain peace with unity, but at the cost of purity. It is easy to obtain peace and purity, but at the cost of unity. And it is easy to obtain unity and purity, but at the cost of peace. Yet this promise is the continuing challenge of church life, if we wish to be faithful to the gospel of Jesus Christ. In a very real sense, it can only be achieved by God's action in our midst.

9

Paul's Gospel in a Nutshell

[15] We ourselves are Jews by birth and not Gentile sinners;
[16] yet we know that a person is justified not by the works
of the law but through faith in Jesus Christ. And we have
come to believe in Christ Jesus, so that we might be justified by faith in Christ, and not by doing the works of the
law, because no one will be justified by the works of the
law. [17] But if, in our effort to be justified in Christ, we
ourselves have been found to be sinners, is Christ then
a servant of sin? Certainly not! [18] But if I build up again
the very things that I once tore down, then I demonstrate
that I am a transgressor. [19] For through the law I died to
the law, so that I might live to God. I have been crucified with Christ; [20] and it is no longer I who live, but it is
Christ who lives in me. And the life I now live in the flesh
I live by faith in the Son of God, who loved me and gave
himself for me. [21] I do not nullify the grace of God; for
if justification comes through the law, then Christ died
for nothing.

IN VERSE 15, WE have a continuation of Paul's criticism of Peter's conduct in Antioch. We have a sense of that by Paul's use of the word "we" as inclusive of Peter and himself. What follows then is what Paul must have argued in his confrontation with Peter. It is the heart of his contention not only with Peter but also with James and the whole Jewish church in Jerusalem.

Paul was born and raised as a Jew, just as were Peter and James. By Jewish understanding that meant they belonged to the people of God whom God had first covenanted with in his promises to Abraham and then later in his commitment to Israel at Mount Sinai. Jews bore witness to their membership in and commitment to this covenant by keeping the commands of Torah, especially those observances that were identity markers of Judaism, like circumcision, the dietary restrictions, and Sabbath keeping.

Gentiles were not included in that covenant with God. They were, therefore, outsiders to the circle of God's people. As outsiders, they were automatically "sinners."

But Paul says to Peter and James and all the other Jewish Christians, "We know that everything has changed as a result of Jesus Christ. We become accepted as members of God's people not by the observing the Jewish Torah, but through faith in Jesus Christ."

When Paul says "we know," he is implying that this is knowledge not only he has, but also Peter and James. He is appealing to common ground among them all. That's why he can accuse Peter of hypocrisy. Peter would agree with this principle just as much as Paul does, but in his behavior, Paul charges, Peter is denying this fundamental principle of the Christian movement.

Now, to be entirely honest, it is not always easy to follow Paul's argument in these verses. His thought is dense. But it is also difficult because he uses words that are sometimes challenging to translate into English. The English words translators usually use have acquired meanings that sometimes vary from the meaning of the Greek words. We read them with our customary English meanings and so miss the point of the Greek.

One example is the word *justify*, which Paul uses four times in this short passage. In English, it is a weighty theological word, weighty with the meaning Protestant theology has given it since the Protestant Reformation. Since Martin Luther, justification has come to mean for Protestants freedom from a guilty conscience and release from God's future condemnation. This freedom comes from placing one's faith in Jesus Christ. It has a largely individualistic orientation.

Now that's not an unbiblical meaning. Certainly Christ brings spiritual freedom to individual believers. But it misses the exact orientation the word *justify* has in this passage of Galatians. There, Paul uses it more in the sense of God declaring that one is in a right relationship with God and is therefore included in God's people. It has a much more social or communal orientation rather than an individual orientation.

Keep in mind that throughout this letter the concern is over the relationship between Jewish believers and Gentile believers within the community of Christianity. Who belongs to the people of God, and on what basis? Paul says that he knows and that Peter also knows one belongs to the people of God through faith in Jesus Christ. There is, therefore, as he will spell out later in chapter 3, equality between the two groups of believers. There is no place for a spiritual segregation. This is, in fact, the central theological affirmation of the letter.

There is another translation difficulty in this passage that has agitated biblical scholars in recent decades in particular. In verse 16 of the New Revised Standard Version that I have been using, Paul says, "We know that a person is justified not by the works of the law but through faith in Jesus Christ."

In Greek, the words that the NRSV translates as "faith in Jesus Christ" are the three words *pistis Jesou Christou*. The word *pistis* is the Greek word for *faith*. But it can also be translated *faithfulness*. The words *Jesou Christou* in Greek are in the genitive case, which would generally be translated as "of Jesus Christ."

But in what sense should we understand the word "of?" If it is a genitive of an object, then it is referring to the content of what one is placing one's faith in. It should be rightly translated "faith in Jesus Christ," for Jesus Christ is the object of one's faith. But if it is a genitive of a subject, then Jesus Christ is the subject or agent who exercises faith. Then it should be rightly translated as the "faith (or faithfulness) of Jesus Christ," meaning the faith (or faithfulness) that Jesus exercised in his life and death.

The King James Version translates the phrase as "faith of Jesus Christ." The Revised Standard Version, the New Revised Standard Version, and the New International Version, however, translate it as "faith in Jesus Christ." Their translation is reflective of the standard interpretation of Paul's thought that has prevailed in most Protestant circles since the Reformation.

If the first translation is correct, then Paul is saying we are justified (or saved, to use another favorite Protestant term) by Jesus Christ's life of faithfulness shown to God, a faithfulness that included a trusting acceptance of his death by crucifixion as part of God's will for him. Christ then becomes the truly and only faithful Israelite. It is because of his faithfulness that we all share in the liberation he brings. The work of salvation is Christ's work, not ours.

If the second translation is correct, then Paul is saying we are justified (or saved) by placing our trusting faith in Jesus Christ, rather than relying on our keeping the observances of Torah or any other religious observances.

I incline to accept the first translation as the correct one. I do so because it is easy, if we go with the second translation, to subtly fall into the trap of thinking that placing my faith in Jesus Christ is itself a good work that saves me. The first translation keeps my focus on justification (or salvation) as purely a gift from God, a gift of God's grace.

However, I still must confront the question that maybe, just maybe, the ambiguity in the Greek is deliberate, for in the outworking of Paul's theology, both translations express a truth. Here is where, if we do not read Greek, we need to pay attention to a diversity of translations to sense the fullness of Paul's thought.

If Christians do not observe the Torah in their behavior, are they not then automatically placing themselves in the category of sinners? That would have been the logical conclusion of those Jewish Christians who argued that Gentile Christians must live by the regulations laid down by Torah. If that is what faith in Christ is doing for Gentile Christians, is not Christ then becoming an agent for the advancement of sin rather than its diminishment?

This may have been the charge the Judaizers were making. If they were, Paul is horrified by the charge. He responds in Greek with the words *me genoito,* which the NRSV translates as *certainly not!* This is a strong expression of rejection, expressing the depth of his disgust at the charge.

So what is happening when a Christian places his or her trust in Jesus Christ? Here's where we come to the central affirmation of Paul's theology:

> [19] For through the law I died to the law, so that I might live to God. I have been crucified with Christ; [20] and it is no longer I who live, but it is Christ who lives in me. And the life I now live in the flesh I live by faith in the Son of God, who loved me and gave himself for me.

First, it is important to notice that Paul switches pronouns from "we" to "I." What he is writing is a theological truth applicable to all Christians, but one he learned himself from his own experience as a Christian. Verses 19–20, therefore, become something more than a statement of an abstract theological principle. They state Paul's own personal experience.

He had been a zealot in his campaign to uphold the supremacy of Torah against the dangers presented by the new Christian movement. But as a result of his personal encounter with Christ, he had undergone a thorough reorientation of his thinking and his values. So thorough was this reorientation that he could talk about having died to Torah, so he could live for God and God's new work.

For Paul, he experienced his Christian life as a dying and rising. That experience is expressed in the sacrament of baptism. Baptism, as an expression of faith, united the believer with Jesus so that the believer is united as well with Jesus's crucifixion and resurrection.

Paul never said this more clearly than he does in Romans 6:3–4:

> Do you not know that all of us who have been baptized into Christ Jesus were baptized into his death? Therefore we have been buried with him by baptism into death, so that, just as Christ was raised from the dead by the glory of the Father, so we too might walk in newness of life.

But this union with Christ in his crucifixion and resurrection is not just a one-time experience, a one-time act of baptism. It is an ongoing experience of the Christian life.

This comes through clearly when we read Paul's statement "I have been crucified with Christ." In Greek, the verb tense is not a simple past tense. The words "have been crucified" are written in the perfect tense. The perfect tense expresses an action that takes place in the past, but that continues to extend or have an impact into the present. I like the way the biblical scholar James D. G. Dunn translates the meaning. "I have been nailed to the cross with Christ, and am still hanging there with him."[1]

The Christian's union with Christ in his death may begin at the moment of faith (expressed concretely in the act of baptism), but it does not end there. That union with Christ's death continues day in and day out throughout the Christian's whole life if he or she has truly placed trust in Jesus Christ.

As a result, Christ lives within us. There is a new animating force at work in our lives. Elsewhere, Paul will call this force the Holy Spirit, but it is always the Spirit conferred by Christ. If we live by the Spirit, our lives will undergo an ongoing transformation that will express itself in changed behavior and feelings. Paul will explain this in greater detail in chapters 5–6 of his Letter to the Galatians.

There is to all this some sense of the Christian life being lived in imitation of Jesus. Jesus becomes the model for the way we are called to live. But there seems to be much more going on in Paul's language than just Jesus modeling good behavior for us. There is

---

1. Dunn, *Epistle to the Galatians*, 144.

a sense in which Jesus truly lives within us. Some have called this Paul's Christ mysticism. That may not be the most accurate way to name Paul's thought, but it does express for us the insight that, for Paul, Jesus is more than just another great guru or teacher.

Paul is realistic enough not to believe that the Christian life lifts us automatically out of the realm of ordinary life—that in-this-world, bodily existence he means by the word *flesh*. That existence is largely egocentric, focused on self-survival and self-fulfillment. As a result of their undergoing a crucifixion with Christ, the lives of Christians also undergo a constant and progressive reorientation. As they grow more mature spiritually, they live less from egocentrism and more by faith in the Son of God, who not only modeled the new life but also gives the power to live it through the Holy Spirit that lives within them.[2]

Then comes a note of beautiful grace. Paul talks about placing our faith in the Son of God "who loved me and gave himself for me." Here we get a sense of the awe that Paul feels about Jesus. All Jesus taught and did was motivated by his love for us—a love that would not balk even at the prospect of dying for us—so that we might enter into the life of God. Here in the midst of some high-flying theology, Paul steps out of abstract theology to touch upon the emotional heart of the Christian gospel. That heart is the amazing love of God for us.

Grace is the reality that God is *for* us, despite everything we may think or feel. Here, Paul is at one with the evangelist writing the Gospel of John:

> For God so loved the world that he gave his only Son, so that everyone who believes in him may not perish but may have eternal life. (John 3:16)

This is the grace that is at work in the gospel. In other letters, contemplation of this grace will evoke ecstatic expressions of adoration from the apostle:

---

2. I say more about how this happens in practice in my theological reflection, "The Spiritual Revolution in One Single Word," which begins on page 139.

O the depth of the riches and the wisdom and knowledge of God! How unsearchable are his judgments and how inscrutable his ways! . . . To whom be the glory forever. Amen. (Rom 11:33, 36)

10

Theological Reflection
Who's Lord? Torah or Christ?

FOLLOWING THE LEAD OF Martin Luther, it has become customary since the Reformation to read the dissension in the Galatian
churches as being over whether our salvation comes from good
works or from faith. This reads the insistence of the Judaizers that
the Gentile Christians live by the Jewish Torah as a fall back into
the righteousness of good works. This position contends that we
earn our salvation by our good behavior.

I disagree with this reading of the Galatian debate. It not only
misreads the Letter to the Galatians, but it also misrepresents the
Judaism that Paul had lived out during his life as a Pharisee. For
Saul the Pharisee, before his encounter with Jesus Christ, Torah
was not a complicated legal system that earned him his righteous
standing with God. It was something different.

HOW TORAH PRESENTS THE PURPOSE OF TORAH

Here we need to pay close attention to how Torah is presented to
us in the Old Testament. Torah is given to Israel as part of the

exodus experience. Its significance must be interpreted within that context.

God does not give the Torah to Israel *before* its liberation out of Egyptian slavery. Instead, Torah is given *after* Israel has been set free.

God does not give the Torah to Moses when he calls Moses at the burning bush on Mount Sinai. He does not say to Moses: "Go to my people of Israel in Egypt and give them this set of laws. If they follow them obediently, I will come and rescue them out of slavery. But I will not free them until they show themselves meriting the gift of freedom."

If God had done something like that, then Israel would have indeed earned its liberation by its good behavior. This would have been salvation by works of righteousness.

But that is not what happens in the Exodus story. God first frees Israel from slavery. He then brings Israel to Mount Sinai where the scriptural text tells us God begins to give to Israel the Torah. Israel's liberation is a gift of God's grace. That liberation comes not because of any good behavior on Israel's part. It comes because of God's faithfulness to the promise he had made to Abraham, Isaac, and Jacob. God is fulfilling his promise.

Now that Israel has been set free, it runs the risk, however, of falling back into some new form of oppression unless it lives a way of life that will maintain the freedom God has given. It is for this benevolent purpose that God gives Israel the Torah. By remembering the story that Torah tells and by living in the way that Torah lays out, Israel will best preserve the freedom it has been given. Israel will flourish as a free people.

If Israel departs from living by Torah, Israel will run the risk of falling back into the patterns of life that maintained their life of slavery in Egypt. Israel will lose all the blessings God conferred upon them. This risk is summed up in the threat of exile.

A HISTORICAL PATTERN: FREEDOM RETURNING TO TYRANNY

Now, all this makes sense if we look at the repeated pattern of revolutions in human history. Take the French Revolution as an example. The revolution overthrew the oppressive Bourbon monarchy, which ushered in a period of chaos that led inexorably first to the Terror, then to the dictatorship of Napoleon Bonaparte. In the end, the revolution overthrew one tyranny only to reestablish another tyranny in its place.

That pattern has been repeated in many revolutions in history. We see it exemplified in the Russian Revolution of 1917 and the Chinese Communist Revolution. Most recently we have seen it repeated in many of the revolutions launched by the Arab Spring in the Middle East.

There's a reason why this pattern repeats itself over and over again. Unless the revolutionaries implement a new pattern of exercising power, they will inevitably fall into old patterns of exercising power. And those old patterns will only reestablish the old oppression under a new name. This is the insight that lies at the heart of George Orwell's dystopian novel *Animal Farm*. If a revolution is to succeed in ushering in freedom on a lasting basis, then it must set in place a new style of exercising power that will support the maintenance of freedom.

That is what I see God doing in the Old Testament when God gives Israel its Torah. God is graciously setting out a vision of human relationships, of human communal life, and of the human-divine relationship that will nurture and support Israel in its new life of freedom.

By living by this Torah, Israel will be showing God, the world, and itself its commitment to the covenantal relationship God has established with it. Israel does not use faithfulness to the Torah to earn its salvation. Rather it lives by Torah in part out of gratitude to God for the liberated life God has given it and in part as a way of maintain the life of freedom God has graciously bestowed upon it.

As a result, living by Torah becomes central to the life of Judaism. It is the way Israel shows its faithfulness to its gracious God. In a sense, Torah became lord in the life of Jews because it expressed the will of their true Lord, the gracious God who gave it. And so if one was to be a faithful member of the family of Abraham, one lived in a way that was faithful to the will of Abraham's God as expressed in the Torah.

THE CENTRAL QUESTION CHRISTIANS MUST DECIDE

Now here's where the issue intersects with the life of those churches in Galatia. The question at the heart of the dissension, as Paul saw it, was the question: Who or what is lord in the life of the Christian community? Is it the Jewish Torah or is it Jesus Christ?

How the early church was to answer this question was to have enormous consequences for Christianity.

If Torah is lord in the Christian community, then Christianity not only grows out of Judaism, but also remains a sect, albeit a rather unorthodox sect, of Judaism. Christianity remains a part of the old covenant between God and Israel. As Paul saw it, that was the logical outworking of the position advocated by the Judaizers who were promoting their views in the Galatian churches.

For Paul, however, the central Christian confession is that Jesus is Lord (See Rom 10:9, 1 Cor 12:3, and Phil 2:11). If Christ is Lord, then Christianity represents a new way in which God is working with human beings. Christianity is grounded in Judaism. From Judaism it draws some of its most central convictions about God. But Christianity becomes something different from Judaism.

In this view, what God has inaugurated in Jesus Christ is a new covenant with humanity (in Latin, a new testament). This new covenant (the new testament) grows out of the old covenant God established with Israel, but it represents a new covenant that embraces not only Jews but also Gentiles.

Which is it? Is Torah lord, or is Jesus Christ lord? The Christian church ultimately adopted the position of Paul. As a result, over the course of several decades, Judaism and Christianity parted ways. They became separate religions.

Since in Christianity, Jesus Christ is Lord, not Torah, then Torah becomes subordinate to Christ. For Paul, therefore, Christians, especially Gentile Christians, have no obligation to live by Torah. They are free of Torah, not because Torah has become oppressive, but because Torah has outlived its reason for being. In fact, as Paul sees it, if Christians continue to live by Torah, then they are cutting themselves off from Christ. Here is the seed ground for the rise of a New Testament (as a book) to supplement the Old Testament (as a book).

For Judaism, on the other hand, Torah remains supreme, as it has been for the last two thousand years in rabbinic Judaism. Since the destruction of the temple in AD 70, the study and living of Torah has been the essence of Judaism. In turn, that led to the development of another supplement to the Old Testament, the Talmud, which seeks to interpret Torah in a way that it speaks to every aspect of life.

We modern Christians do not fully realize how astounding it is that Paul argues the position he does in the Letter to the Galatians. Paul was born a Jew and educated as a Pharisee. Pharisees were the most zealous of Jews in living out the Torah. Pharisees constituted the main contingent among those Jewish leaders who created rabbinic Judaism after the fall of Jerusalem in AD 70. Orthodox Judaism today represents their greatest and most admirable achievement.

As a good Pharisee, Paul, before his conversion, persecutes the Christian movement because he sees the Christian church threatening the primacy of Torah in the life of Judaism.

In the gospels, Jesus's chief opponents are the Pharisees. They are opponents not primarily because of Jesus exposing their occasional hypocrisy but because of their zeal for keeping Torah. Jesus threatens this primacy of Torah by some of the actions and claims he makes. For example, when some Pharisees challenge Jesus because his disciples are picking and eating grains of wheat on the Sabbath, the gospel of Mark quotes Jesus as saying, "The Sabbath is made for humankind, and not humankind for the Sabbath; so the Son of Man is lord even of the Sabbath" (Mark 2:27–28). This was to confront the issue in early Christianity bluntly.

What changes Paul's viewpoint is his encounter with the risen Jesus on the Damascus Road. As we saw in my first theological reflection on Paul's conversion, Paul recognizes the vision as a revelation of God. Note that he says, "Who are you, Lord?" What threw his life into total confusion was the answer he received: "I am Jesus, whom you are persecuting."

Paul hears God speaking through Jesus. He is also told that in persecuting the church, Paul is persecuting Jesus, which makes no sense unless there is a profound union between Jesus and the Christian church.

This encounter has an outcome that turns Paul's life and mind-set upside down. He realizes God is at work in this new Christian movement. It is not apostasy, but the leading edge of God's movement in the world. That means Torah has been relativized. In the Letter to the Galatians, we see Paul unpacking the import of that insight.

WHAT CAN WE LEARN TODAY FROM THE GALATIAN DEBATE

Now as you read all this, you may be saying to yourself: this is all very interesting as an analysis of the early development of Christianity, but what relevance does it have for modern-day Christians?

For one, it can help us to regain a more positive view of Judaism than most Christians have had in the past. We see the Old Testament Torah and the Judaism that grows out of it not as some kind of oppressive religion grounded in an understanding of salvation by works. No, we see in the Old Testament the same God of grace at work as we see in the New Testament in Jesus Christ. Torah is a gracious and good gift of God, as even Paul will confess later in the Letter to the Galatians. Judaism is as much a religion of grace as is Christianity.

The debate between Judaism and Christianity is a debate over what or who is lord in the life of faithfulness. Is it Torah or is it Jesus Christ? As we find in so many of the debates within the Old Testament, the debate is one within the circle of God's people, not one between an inside group and an outside group. Even though we Christians answer differently from our Jewish brothers and sisters, we can honor each other as partners in an inter-family dialogue.

The second thing is that we Christians need to remember we also possess what I might call a Christian Torah. Torah in the Old Testament lays out the stories of God's gracious acts with Israel and the way of life that honors that grace of God expressed in his choice of Israel to be his people. As Judaism develops, Torah too grows to embrace not just the five books of Moses, but all the interpretations of God's will that constitute the tradition of Judaism.

Christians, too, tell a story of God's gracious acts on our behalf. We call it gospel. We seek to understand this story and its implications through the development of Christian doctrine. We also have an understanding of the way Christians need to live to honor this life of freedom that God has conferred upon us in Jesus Christ. We have expressed this understanding in the multifaceted ethical traditions of our Christian faith and in those practices we call spiritual disciplines. We have developed structures for guiding our worship. We call them our Christian liturgies.

I want to contend that these doctrines, ethics, disciplines, and liturgies constitute our Christian Torah. We ground them in Scripture just as rabbinic Judaism grounds Torah (and by extension, the Talmud) in the revelation of God given through the patriarchs, Moses, and the prophets.

Just as different schools for interpreting Torah have arisen in Judaism, so too Christianity has its differing traditions of understanding the Christian Torah. We see that in the differing theological and denominational parties that constitute contemporary Christianity. We see our theological constructs not as establishing a works righteousness religion but as expressing what faithfulness to God's grace looks like in daily living.

Yet those differing parties can be just as excluding of those with whom they disagree as were those Judaizers who broke up table fellowship in the church in Antioch. Too many Christian denominations still uphold closed Communion policies. Table fellowship at the Lord's Supper is only extended to those who agree with their doctrines and practices.

If Paul were to appear suddenly in our churches today, might he not once again raise the question: What or who is lord? Is it your exclusive denominational or theological Torah, or even the Bible, or is it Jesus Christ?

11

An Appeal to Religious Experience

GALATIANS 3:1-5

> [1] You foolish Galatians! Who has bewitched you? It was
> before your eyes that Jesus Christ was publicly exhibited
> as crucified! [2] The only thing I want to learn from you is
> this: Did you receive the Spirit by doing the works of the
> law or by believing what you heard? [3] Are you so fool-
> ish? Having started with the Spirit, are you now ending
> with the flesh? [4] Did you experience so much for noth-
> ing?—if it really was for nothing. [5] Well then, does God
> supply you with the Spirit and work miracles among you
> by your doing the works of the law, or by your believing
> what you heard?

IN THE FIRST TWO chapters of Galatians, Paul lays out the lines
of the debate that is troubling the Christian movement. How are
Gentiles to be accepted into the Christian community? Must they,
in effect, become Jewish in order to be Christian, or are Gentiles
accepted on another basis?

At the end of chapter 2, Paul makes his own position in the
debate clear:

> We have come to believe in Christ Jesus, so that we might
> be justified by faith in Christ, and not by doing the works
> of the law [Torah], because no one will be justified by the
> works of the law. (Gal 2:16)

For Paul, all believers, whether Jewish by origin or Gentile,
are justified before God on one basis, and one basis alone: faith in
Jesus Christ.[1] This is his position in the debate.

With chapter 3, Paul begins his defense of his position. We
shall see that he uses a variety of rhetorical strategies to support
his position. They include personal invective as well as rabbinic
and Hellenistic approaches to interpreting the Old Testament.
With these opening verses of chapter 3, he launches into his first
strategy.

Among the various appeals Paul will make as he proceeds,
I find this one the most curious of all, for it is a frank and direct
appeal to the Galatian believers' religious experience. How did
they receive the Holy Spirit? By practicing Torah or by hearing the
gospel with faith?

What is curious about this argument is his assumption that
his hearers will know exactly what he is talking about. His argument would carry no water if his hearers had scratched their heads
at this point and asked: what do you mean about receiving the
Spirit?

Apparently these Galatian Christians had some powerful
religious experience that they knew without question was an experience of the Holy Spirit. It must have been common among the
believers. In verse 5, Paul speaks of God supplying the Spirit. The
English word *supply* translates the Greek verb *epichoregeo*. In classical Greek, this verb was used to describe the action of a rich man
in paying for the expenses of mounting a theatrical play. It was also
used to describe the action of a husband providing for his wife.

---

1. Here I follow the NRSV in its wording "faith in Christ," as that is the
way the NRSV translates the ambiguous Greek phrase *pistis Christou*. But as
we noticed previously, the Greek can also be translated as "the faithfulness of
Christ." By that alternate translation, what justifies us is Christ's faithfulness,
which we gain access to through our faith in Christ.

What the verb does is remind the Galatians of God's character. He is the benefactor who is providing generously for their spiritual welfare.

What we modern readers would like to know is just exactly how these Galatian believers experienced the Spirit. Did they experience the Spirit in the kind of emotional phenomena that today we associate with the Pentecostal tradition? Did they experience the Spirit in terms of dramatically changed lives, maybe in terms of a dramatically changed consciousness or dramatically changed behavior?

Or did they experience the Spirit in terms of witnessing miracles in their midst, possibly dramatic healings? In verse five, Paul makes a reference to miracles. Is that how they had experienced the Spirit? Or did they experience the Spirit in all of these various ways?

The text does not make it clear just how the Galatians experienced the Spirit. But that they had some kind of vivid experience of the Spirit is certain. Otherwise, Paul could never have used this argument in his debate with them.

It was a very persuasive argument, especially for the Gentile converts. Soon, Paul will launch into a defense of his position by appealing to Scripture (meaning the Old Testament). Paul will show how carefully he has read and absorbed the message of Scripture. The new Gentile converts, however, probably would not have shared that intimate familiarity with the Old Testament. Unless they had been God-fearers for some years, attending the synagogue regularly, most of the Gentile converts would have had a sketchy knowledge of the Old Testament, if any knowledge at all.

But all of the believers in the churches, whether Gentile or Jewish by origin, would have experienced the spiritual phenomena to which Paul is appealing. Their experience would have ratified what Paul was saying. Maybe that is why Paul addresses them as "foolish Galatians." How could they be so blind to the import of their own religious experiences?

I'm fascinated by Paul's rhetorical turn in these verses because I question that this kind of argument would work with many

Christians in churches today. I suspect that most Christians today (unless they come out of a Pentecostal environment) would have no idea what Paul was talking about. The Holy Spirit is simply not a vivid experience for many believers today.

Is that because our churches have done a very effective job at quenching the Holy Spirit? Or is it that we have so identified the Spirit's presence with highly emotional phenomena, like speaking in tongues, that we completely miss the Spirit's presence in other ways? Or is it that we have done such a poor job of teaching about the Spirit that we cannot recognize the Spirit's presence in our midst?

I ask because I wonder what it would be like in our churches if we had such a vivid experience of the Spirit in our individual lives and in our congregational life that we could respond with clarity, conviction, and enthusiasm if Paul stood in our midst and asked: How did you receive the Spirit?

12

An Appeal to Scripture

GALATIANS 3:6-14

[6] Just as Abraham "believed God, and it was reckoned to him as righteousness," [7] so, you see, those who believe are the descendants of Abraham. [8] And the scripture, foreseeing that God would justify the Gentiles by faith, declared the gospel beforehand to Abraham, saying, "All the Gentiles shall be blessed in you." [9] For this reason, those who believe are blessed with Abraham who believed.

[10] For all who rely on the works of the law are under a curse; for it is written, "Cursed is everyone who does not observe and obey all the things written in the book of the law." [11] Now it is evident that no one is justified before God by the law; for "The one who is righteous will live by faith." [12] But the law does not rest on faith; on the contrary, "Whoever does the works of the law will live by them." [13] Christ redeemed us from the curse of the law by becoming a curse for us—for it is written, "Cursed is everyone who hangs on a tree"— [14] in order that in Christ Jesus the blessing of Abraham might come to the

> Gentiles, so that we might receive the promise of the
> Spirit through faith.

IN THE PREVIOUS FIVE verses, Paul grounded his argument in the incontrovertible fact that the Galatian believers received the Holy Spirit. They cannot deny that fact. But have they thought deeply enough about what that implies?

For Paul, their experiences imply nothing less than that they now form a portion of the people of God. God has blessed them with the gift of God's Spirit. They are not outsiders to the people of God anymore. They are insiders, constituent parts.

The early church saw the gift of the Spirit as a sign that the promised new age had dawned. They were experiencing the special blessing associated with the coming age when the Kingdom of God would arrive.

This belief is clear when we read the speech that the apostle Peter gave on Pentecost Day as recorded in Acts 2. Peter quotes the Old Testament prophet Joel, who envisioned the coming of the new age (Joel 2:28–32). It would bring with it an outpouring of God's Spirit upon all flesh. In its original Old Testament context, this would have been read as a promise of the outpouring of God's Spirit upon all of restored Israel. But now that the Spirit was being given to Gentiles, they had to read the phrase "all flesh" in a much broader way.

This outpouring of the Spirit on Gentiles meant that in some surprising way Gentiles had become a part of the family of Abraham. Our understanding of the family of Abraham has to become much more expansive.

So with verse 6, Paul turns his attention to Scripture. What do the Hebrew Scriptures say that is relevant to the crisis in the Galatian churches? And so through the rest of chapter 3 and into chapter 4, Paul will engage in some deft, although also difficult, interpretation of Scripture.

Before we launch into it, let me say a couple of things about Paul's use of Scripture. First, when Paul appeals to Scripture, he is appealing to what we Christians today call the Old Testament. Nothing of the New Testament yet existed. Paul may have written a few letters already, but they were not yet recognized as Holy Scripture. And nothing of the four gospels had been written either. So when we read Paul's appeal to Scripture, we must always be aware that he is turning to the Old Testament as his authoritative texts.

Many Christians today tend to ignore the Old Testament. Some do so because they hold to an ancient misreading of the Old Testament. This misreading contrasted the God of the Old Testament as a God of wrath with the God of the New Testament as a God of love. If I were writing a different book, I would show that this is a misreading of the Hebrew Scriptures.

Some others ignore the Old Testament because they see it as now obsolete, with its many ceremonial laws and its seemingly nationalistic focus on the story of the Jews. This attitude toward the Old Testament has a long history in Christianity, but it too misreads the Old Testament in my opinion.

When Christianity accepted the Old Testament as a part of the Bible along with the New Testament, Christians were saying the two must be constantly read together. If we are to understand the New Testament, we must, I believe, soak ourselves in the language, stories, and theology of the Old Testament. They form two parts of one divine story.

The second thing I need to say is that when we read Paul's appeal to the Old Testament, we may initially think Paul is engaging in some arbitrary proof texting. Is he any different from Christians today who cull texts out the Bible willy-nilly to support whatever theological, political, or social position they espouse?

It is important to remember that Paul was carefully trained in the techniques of biblical interpretation in the rabbinic schools where he spent his youth. We will find that following that training, he engages in some very close reading of the text. In particular, he will sometimes pay very close attention to one particular word in the text. We may be inclined to skip over that word as insignificant. Paul, however, will find individual words in the text as theologically weighty. And so he will make those words critical to his argument.

Also, we will notice that Paul does not engage in random proof-texting, culling here and there texts that support his position. He remains deeply aware of the original context in which his quotations are embedded. So when we read his quotations, we are wise to return to the original Old Testament context to see what broader theological discussion is going on in that original context.

Now let's focus our attention on Paul's appeal to Scripture.

The fact that Gentile believers were experiencing the Holy Spirit was something both sides in the dispute acknowledged. Did that mean, however, that Gentile believers now belonged to the chosen people of God, the people of Israel?

The Judaizers were probably arguing that in order to become a member of God's people, one had to become a son (or daughter) of Abraham. That meant that Gentile converts had to start observing Torah, for it was the observance of Torah that defined the identity of Jews.

In particular, in the Greco-Roman world of Paul's day, four specific behaviors set Jews apart from their Gentile neighbors: male circumcision, observance of the special dietary laws prescribed in the Old Testament, avoidance of sharing the dining table with Gentiles, and a strict observance of the Sabbath rest.

In particular, these Judaizers seemed to have been arguing that male Gentile converts had to be circumcised. Here it seemed that they had the full authority of the Old Testament on their side. The crucial text is found in Genesis 17:9–14:

> And God said to Abraham, "As for you, you shall keep my covenant, you and your descendants after you throughout their generations. This is my covenant, which you shall keep, between me and you and your descendants after you: Every male among you shall be circumcised. You shall be circumcised in the flesh of your foreskins, and it shall be a sign of the covenant between me and you. . . . So shall my covenant be in your flesh an everlasting covenant. Any uncircumcised male who is not circumcised in the flesh of his foreskin shall be cut off from his people; he has broken my covenant."

What could be clearer on the necessity of circumcision? After all, the Bible said so.

But hold on, says Paul. Let's read this divine command in context. That context is the whole Genesis narrative. Note where this command falls in the story of Abraham. (If you are going to follow Paul's argument, you need to go back and read the first twenty chapters of Genesis.)

Before Genesis chapter 17 comes Genesis chapter 15. Let's note what we find there:

> After these things the word of the Lord came to Abram in a vision, "Do not be afraid, Abram, I am your shield; your reward shall be very great." But Abram said, "O Lord God, what will you give me, for I continue childless, and the heir of my house is Eliezer of Damascus?" And Abram said, "You have given me no offspring, and so a slave born in my house is to be my heir." But the word of the Lord came to him, "This man shall not be your heir; no one but your very own issue shall be your heir." He brought him outside and said, "Look toward heaven and count the stars, if you are able to count them." Then he said to him, "So shall your descendants be." And he believed the Lord; and the Lord reckoned it to him as righteousness. (Gen 15:1–6)

In chapter 12 of Genesis, God promised to Abraham that he would give the land of Canaan to Abraham's descendants. But in chapter 12, Abraham is childless. How can God make such a promise when Abraham has no children? That is the theological dilemma Abraham—and we—face when we begin to read chapter 15.

In chapter 15, God reiterates his promise to Abraham, expanding it to include an additional promise that his descendants will be as numerous as the stars in the heavens. God does not ask anything of Abraham in this text. He is asked, in effect, to do nothing but believe in God's promise. And the text says he does. Then comes that crucial sentence: "He [God] reckoned it to him [Abraham] as righteousness."

Paul notices this particular wording. Abraham comes into right relationship with God by believing in God's promises. By its chronological priority in the story of Genesis, Genesis 15 trumps Genesis 17.

The point that Paul draws from this appeal is that the children of Abraham include anyone who believes in God's promises. God takes the initiative in his dealings with Abraham, as God does with us. God's action, therefore, takes priority over anything we do. The person who is in right relationship with God achieves his or her status in God's presence not by anything he or she does, but by simply believing in God's promises, which are fulfilled in Jesus Christ.

Paul then goes even farther back into the text of Genesis. He carries us back to Genesis 12, where God begins his interaction with Abraham. The crucial text is Genesis 12:1–3:

> Now the LORD said to Abram, "Go from your country and your kindred and your father's house to the land that I will show you. And I will make of you a great nation, and I will bless you, and make your name great, so that you will be a blessing. I will bless those who bless you, and him who curses you I will curse; and by you all the families of the earth shall bless themselves."

In this famous call story, God calls Abraham (his original name is Abram) to leave behind his family and social identity and to follow God to a land God will show him. If he does, God makes some astounding promises to Abraham.

What Paul focuses on is the last of those promises. The NRSV translates it as, "by you all the families of the earth shall bless themselves." The original Hebrew can actually be translated in different ways. One alternate translation is, "In you all the nations of the earth shall be blessed." That's how the Greek translation of the Old Testament that the early church used as its authority translates that sentence. And Paul appeals to it.

Here once again, I do not believe Paul is engaging in any crude proof-texting. He is reading Genesis 12 in its own context. The call of Abraham follows almost directly after the story of the

Tower of Babel told in Genesis 11:1–9. That story ends with primordial humanity falling into disunity and being sentenced into a global-wide exile. God's good creation has been fragmented by human sin.

How is God to bring about a restoration of unity and wholeness into his good creation? How is humanity to be reunited into a peaceful and blessed unity? When we read the story of the call of Abraham in this context, we hear the theologian/editor of Genesis making an astounding claim. The call of Abraham is God's response. It starts in process a historical movement that is to end in nothing less that the conferring of God's *shalom* (peace) upon all of humanity, not just Jews alone.

This is how Paul is reading Genesis. In his Pharisaic days, Paul would have read Genesis as promising God's blessing to only faithful Jews. They were the sons of Abraham. But as a result of his encounter with Jesus Christ, Paul reads the Genesis story in a different light. What God was *not* doing in the creation of the people of Israel was creating an exclusive, privileged people in contrast to an excluded, unprivileged people. No, what God was doing was creating a way for *all* of humanity to enter into a privileged relationship with God.

What Paul says, however, will have no persuasive power for you if you are not reading the text of Genesis as closely as he is. Here is an example of how, if we are to understand the New Testament, we must soak ourselves in the Old Testament. The welcoming of Gentiles into the Christian community is part of the fulfillment of God's promise to Abraham.

Inclusion, however, is grounded in faith in Jesus Christ, not in adopting those practices of Torah that identify Jews and exclude Gentiles. In fact, Paul goes on, if you, a Gentile, adopt those practices, obeying the commandments of the Torah cannot bring life.

Jews would have denied this conclusion, citing passages like Deuteronomy 30:11–20. There, Moses says that the commandment he gives to Israel is not too hard for them. Rather, "it is in your mouth and in your heart for you to observe." And in Leviticus 18:5 (a verse Paul will quote in verse 12), God says to Israel, "You shall keep my statutes and my ordinances; by doing so one shall live."

Despite these scriptural citations, Paul will argue that the Torah cannot deliver life. The reason is because the Mosaic law brings a curse on anyone who does not keep it fully. To support his point, Paul returns to the same text that the Jews would have appealed to: Deuteronomy. In Deuteronomy 27:26, he finds Moses also saying, "Cursed is everyone who does not observe and obey all the things written in the book of the law." Instead of finding life in the Torah, you will fall under its curse if you do not practice Torah completely and sincerely.

Paul is saying that no one can fully keep all the commandments of the Torah. If you question Paul's conclusion, then you might want to remember what Jesus says in the Sermon on the Mount. For Jesus, fulfilling the law is not just a matter of actions, but also of the inner dispositions of the heart. We may be able to control our behavior, but we will find it far harder to control the emotions that motivate that behavior.

A right standing in our relationship with God (justification), and therefore life, comes only by faith. This, too, is Old Testament teaching, Paul asserts. In support, he quotes the prophet Habakkuk. In verse 2:4 of that prophet, God says, "The one who is righteous will live by faith."[1]

Paul then goes on to say something extraordinary. Christ frees us from the curse of Torah by becoming a curse for us. A mysterious interchange is at work. Christ becomes the subject of a curse so that we can have the curse lifted off of us.

This statement will strike us as puzzling unless we understand that in Paul's day, at least among Jews, crucifixion was understood

---

1. It is worthwhile to read this verse in its original context as well. Habakkuk speaks at a time when the Babylonian armies are snuffing out Judean independence. The prophets had said this was God's judgment on Judean sin. But Habakkuk responds to God by saying that the Babylonians are even more evil. How can that be justice? God responds to Habakkuk, counseling him to be patient. God has not finished his work. And then comes the critical verse, "The one who is righteous shall live by faith."

as conferring the curse of God upon the one crucified. This was part of the shame and horror that crucifixion had for Jews.

This belief is based upon another passage from Deuteronomy, 21:22–23:

> When someone is convicted of a crime punishable by death and is executed, and you hang him on a tree, his corpse must not remain all night upon the tree; you shall bury him that same day, for anyone hung on a tree is under God's curse. You must not defile the land that the Lord your God is giving you for possession.

In its original context, this passage was seeking to prevent the untended exposure of the body of an executed criminal. It had a compassionate motive behind it. But in Paul's day, this verse was understood as applying to crucifixion. It conferred God's curse on one crucified. So when Jesus died on a cross, it was clear to a traditional Jewish audience that he could not be the Messiah. He bore God's curse.

But for Paul, God overturns that curse by the resurrection of Jesus from the dead. Jesus is vindicated and exalted as Lord over the cosmos. As a result, the blessing God promises to Abraham's descendants does indeed get fulfilled. It is fulfilled in the gift of the Holy Spirit, that very gift that Paul reminds the Galatians they received when they believed.

The Holy Spirit is the promised blessing. If that seems a curious thing to say, keep in mind what the gospel of Luke quotes Jesus as saying. Jesus teaches his disciples about prayer, and ends this session by saying, in Luke 11:11–13:

> Is there anyone among you who, if your child asks for a fish, will give a snake instead of a fish? Or if the child asks for an egg, will give a scorpion? If you then, who are evil, know how to give good gifts to your children, how much more will the heavenly Father give the Holy Spirit to those who ask him!

To understand how startling what Jesus says here is, we need to compare it with how the Gospel of Matthew (7:9–11) quotes this very same teaching from Jesus. Matthew ends with Jesus saying, "How much more will your Father in heaven give good things to those who ask him!" But Luke seems to change those words *good things* to the Holy Spirit. The Holy Spirit is the very essence and the sum-all of *good things*.

Once we begin to pay attention to these passages in the New Testament, we begin to recognize something of the high value these early Christians placed upon the gift of the Holy Spirit. When later Trinitarian doctrine understands the Holy Spirit as being fully God, then we begin to understand that the gift of the Holy Spirit is nothing less than the gift of God's own self to us. If we have God, we have all good things.

13

Security in the Promise

GALATIANS 3:15-22

[15] Brothers and sisters, I give an example from daily life: once a person's will has been ratified, no one adds to it or annuls it. [16] Now the promises were made to Abraham and to his offspring; it does not say, "And to offsprings," as of many; but it says, "And to your offspring," that is, to one person, who is Christ. [17] My point is this: the law, which came four hundred thirty years later, does not annul a covenant previously ratified by God, so as to nullify the promise. [18] For if the inheritance comes from the law, it no longer comes from the promise; but God granted it to Abraham through the promise.

[19] Why then the law? It was added because of transgressions, until the offspring would come to whom the promise had been made; and it was ordained through angels by a mediator. [20] Now a mediator involves more than one party; but God is one.

[21] Is the law then opposed to the promises of God? Certainly not! For if a law had been given that could make alive, then righteousness would indeed come

through the law. [22] But the scripture has imprisoned all
things under the power of sin, so that what was promised
through faith in Jesus Christ might be given to those who
believe.

IN THE PREVIOUS PASSAGE, Paul argued that Gentile believers
can have confidence they are numbered among the children of
Abraham because of their faith in Jesus Christ. They do not need
to obey the dictates of Torah for security in their status.

Their status as children of Abraham rests upon God's promise, not upon anything they do. Their status is a gift of God's good
favor. They can, therefore, relax and not feel anxious.

They can trust in God's promise because it cannot be changed.
To support his point, Paul turns to an analogy from ordinary life.
When a person makes a will, no one else can then go in and change
the provisions of the will. The will-maker can, of course, but that
is not the point Paul is calling attention to. His point is that no one
else can.

In an analogous way, God has made a promise to Abraham
and to Abraham's descendants. We can trust in that promise because God does not revoke his promises.

Paul then returns to the Old Testament to substantiate his
point. Here, however, he engages in some typically rabbinic exegesis. We may find it peculiar reasoning, but it would not have been
considered peculiar in the schools in which he was trained, for it
involved a very close reading of the Scripture text.

In reading the promises God makes to Abraham in Genesis,
Paul notices something unusual about the wording. In Genesis
12:7, for example, God promises the land of Canaan to Abraham
and his descendants. He does so in this wording: "To your offspring I will give this land." This promise is repeated in Genesis
13:15 with parallel wording.

In Hebrew and in the Greek translation that Paul would have
been quoting, the word the NRSV translates as *offspring* is the
word *seed*. In both languages that would have been understood to
refer to descendants. But Paul notices that in the text, it says *seed* in
the singular, not *seeds* in the plural. From that, Paul concludes that

the promise is made to Abraham and to one and only one of his descendants. That one seed, he says, is Christ, in whom believers have placed their trust. It is through Christ that believers receive their inheritance of the Holy Spirit.

If this is the case, Paul's audience could have rightly asked the question, "Then why did God give the Torah to Israel?" Paul gives his answer. It has two parts. The first part he will answer in verses 19 and 20. The second part he will answer in verses 23 through 25.

The first answer is that the Torah was given "because of transgressions, until the offspring would come to whom the promise was given." "Because of transgressions" is a cryptic phrase. It can be read in at least two different ways. One is that the Torah ends up making unconscious sins conscious. The Torah exposes the evil intent of the inner heart. So now when we sin, we do so with a conscious guilt because we know what we do is wrong.

But the phrase can be read in a second way. "Because of transgressions" may also be a reference to all the cultic regulations, especially the sacrificial system, that we find specified in the Torah. Those regulations give a means by which Israel can deal with its sin and establish restoration or atonement (at-one-ment) in their relationship with God. That understanding makes sense of the additional wording "until the offspring will come." It sees the sacrifice of Christ on the cross as providing the final and complete atonement that makes the cultic regulations of the Old Testament now unnecessary.

Paul also degrades the status of the Torah by indicating that it was given to Israel 430 years later than the promise was given to Abraham. That figure is based upon what is said in Exodus 12:40–41.

Furthermore, Paul alludes to the common Jewish belief in his time that God gave the Torah to Moses, not directly but through the intermediary service of angels. Moses, in turn, shares the Torah with Israel. However, God speaks his promise to Abraham directly without any intermediary. This gives exalted status to the promise.

This does not mean the Torah contradicts the promise. The Torah has a purpose, but that purpose is not to give life in the way faith in Jesus Christ does.

14

A New Era Begins

GALATIANS 3:23–29

[23] Now before faith came, we were imprisoned and guarded under the law until faith would be revealed. [24] Therefore the law was our disciplinarian until Christ came, so that we might be justified by faith. [25] But now that faith has come, we are no longer subject to a disciplinarian, [26] for in Christ Jesus you are all children of God through faith. [27] As many of you as were baptized into Christ have clothed yourselves with Christ. [28] There is no longer Jew or Greek, there is no longer slave or free, there is no longer male and female; for all of you are one in Christ Jesus. [29] And if you belong to Christ, then you are Abraham's offspring, heirs according to the promise.

As MENTIONED ABOVE, WHEN Paul is asked why God gave Israel the Torah if the status of being children of Abraham rests upon God's promise, Paul says the Torah serves two functions. He highlights its first function in that ambiguous phrase "because of transgressions" in verse 19.

But Torah serves a second purpose as well. Paul highlights that in this passage, saying that Torah was designed (in the words used by the NRSV translation) to be our disciplinarian until Christ came when we might be justified by faith.

The word *disciplinarian* translates a specific Greek word. That word is *paidagogus*. This Greek word refers to a special servant who would have been found in an affluent or moderately affluent Greek family. In such a family, a son would be given an education until he reached the age of maturity when he could assume his adult responsibilities.

While he was in this period of education, his parents would put him under the charge of a family servant called the *paidagogus*. The *paidagogus* functioned as the caretaker and guardian of the young boy during his training years. He would walk with the boy to school to ensure safe travel. He cared for the boy's well-being. But he did much more. He was also in charge of the boy's moral education. When the boy reached the age of maturity, the *paidagogus* dropped away and ceased to play any function in the young man's life.

Greek Christians in the Galatians churches would have been quite familiar with this figure. So when Paul compares the role of Torah to that of a *paidagogus*, his language would have resonated with his Gentile listeners.

This understanding of the role of Torah has support in the Old Testament even though Paul does not cite that support in this discussion. But if he had wanted, Paul could have again called upon a close reading of the Exodus story to support his point. In the Exodus story, the Ten Commandments and the rest of Torah are given to Israel after its liberation from bondage in Egypt, not before.

If you think that keeping Torah establishes your status with God (and you earn merit that is rewarded by your being liberated from bondage), then you misread the Exodus story. God does not give Torah to Israel with the stipulation that if you keep God's commandments faithfully, then God will come and free you from bondage.

No, Torah is given after the liberation has been accomplished. Pharaoh has been defeated; Israel has crossed the Red Sea. Now that Israel has been set free, how is Israel to live in such a way that it does not fall back into bondage again, does not surrender its freedom?

Torah does not establish Israel as God's sons and daughters; that status God has given to Israel even before its liberation (see especially Exod 4:22–23). What Torah does is guide Israel in the kinds of behavior that will enable it to preserve and maintain its freedom once it has been set free.

But the extraordinary thing Paul sees about this gift of Torah is that it is a temporary gift. It is given for guiding the life of Israel during those long centuries before Jesus Christ arrives, when God's people will finally be justified (find their right status with God) through faith in Christ. In this respect, Torah serves a role analogous to that of a *paidagogus*.

Now, however, since the Galatian believers have placed their faith in Christ, they are no longer minor sons and daughters of Abraham. They are now full adults and therefore free of the constraints of the *paidagogus*. Paul makes this conviction absolutely clear in verse 26 when he says to the Galatian believers, "In Christ Jesus, you are all children of God through faith."

We, like Paul, must become close readers of the Scripture text. Notice that Paul says these Galatian believers are children of God *in* Christ Jesus. That little word *in* is a tiny word, only two letters long in both English and in Greek. Yet it is weighty in theology. To share in the blessings promised to Abraham and his descendants, we must be *in* the *seed*, which is Christ.

How does one come to be in Christ? By faith, says Paul. By a faith or trust in Jesus Christ, which expresses itself in the act of undergoing baptism. As verse 27 makes clear, we come to be incorporated into Christ, we "put on" Christ like a new garment in the act of baptism.

Among American Protestants, especially those whose heritage grows out of the revivalist movements of the nineteenth and twentieth centuries, Paul's thought will seem a bit strange. They tend to see the decisive turning point in the Christian's life as that moment when one confesses one's sin and one's need for a savior. And then one goes on to claim Jesus as one's personal Lord and Savior. Classically, this is done by saying the Sinner's Prayer. It constitutes the definition of being born again.

For such Christians, baptism is just a symbol of one's commitment to Christ. It is an act of obedience that responds to Christ's command to his apostles to baptize. But it does not make any significant change in one's spiritual life.

If we are to understand the significance of baptism for Paul, we must understand this rite of the church in the context in which Paul is writing. We do not know much about how the rite of baptism was conducted in Paul's day. The first accounts of the rite of baptism in the early church come in the second century, long after Paul. But what we know about those rites gives us some hints as to the importance and methods of baptism in the apostolic church.

Baptism was a decisive turning point in the Christian's life. In the rite of baptism, a person renounced sin, evil, and the devil. One then professed one's belief in and allegiance to Jesus Christ as Lord and Savior.

The rite began with the new convert taking off his or her street clothes, then entering the baptismal pool or a river, being immersed in the water by a representative of the church, and then after one emerged from the water, being dressed in a white robe or garment and led into the church congregation for one's first participation in the Eucharist (the Lord's Supper).

When Paul refers to *putting on* Christ in verse 27, he may be alluding to this custom of dressing the newly baptized in the white garment (if that happened in the churches he founded). In the early church, Easter Eve was the customary day for baptism. So we today retain a vestige of this custom in our modern-day custom of wearing new clothes or hats to an Easter service.

Now for everyone in the ancient world, baptism was the decisive point where a person moved from his or her identity as a Jew or pagan and assumed the new identity of a Christian. Before baptism, one might believe in Christian doctrines and practice

Christian morality, but one was not yet regarded as a Christian. Such unbaptized people who hung around a church were not all that different from the God-fearers who attended the Jewish synagogue. God-fearers might be attracted to Judaism and practice some of its rites and laws, but until a man was circumcised he remained a Gentile.

In a similar way, a Jew or pagan could have a curiosity in Christianity and attend services, but until that decisive moment when he or she was baptized, he or she remained a Jew or Gentile in the eyes of both Christians as well as in the eyes of outsiders. All that changed decisively when one underwent baptism. Everyone, both Christians and non-Christians, now regarded that person as a Christian.

We can compare it to the ceremony of naturalization when a foreign citizen becomes a citizen of the United States. A foreigner may live in the United States for years, buy property here, and pay taxes, but he or she is not regarded as a citizen until he or she proclaims allegiance to the United States in the naturalization ceremony. After it, one is not only regarded as an American citizen; one also enjoys the privileges as well as the responsibilities of citizenship.

So when one was baptized in the early church, one was undergoing a decisive change of status. For most of these new Christians, it must have been a deeply emotional, life-changing experience. In that respect, we can see the act of baptism as an expression of saving faith comparable to what American evangelicals call the born-again experience. Both are valid expressions of faith, in which one is "putting on" Christ.

But there is more going on in baptism. In the ancient church as in modern churches, baptism is not only an expression of faith, but it is the rite by which a new believer is united with the community of faith, the church, which Paul regards as the body of Christ. It offers the spiritual doorway into that community. When one "puts on" Christ, one also puts on the church, for a profound unity unites Christ and the community of his disciples.

From this fact, Paul draws a revolutionary conclusion. Baptism means we are not only united with Christ and with the Christian community, but it also establishes a radical equality among all Christian believers. No more are the age-old status distinctions of human society and nature valid. The distinctions between Jew and Gentile, between slave and free person, between male and female, become obsolete in the life of the church. In their place is established a radical equality.

Paul will make clear in other letters that the only distinctions valid in the body of Christ are distinctions of function, not of status. One may function in the church as a pastor, deacon, prophet, compassionate caregiver, donor, or teacher, but these are all distinctions in function. Issues of superiority or inferiority, as we experience them outside the body of Christ in the societies in which we live, no longer have validity in the life of the church.

This radical equality would have offended many in the early church, and probably many among those Galatian believers to whom Paul was writing. The Jewish believer, the free person believer, the male believer, would all have likely felt superior to the Gentile believer, the slave believer, and the female believer. Paul's thought would have punctured all attempts to establish different classes in the membership of the church.

To be frank, Christians have found it very hard to live out Paul's vision of equality. We have example upon example in the long, two-thousand-year history of Christianity. Let me cite just a few examples: the growth of hierarchy in the organization of the church,[1] the virtual two-class system that keeps emerging in churches where clergy are spiritually elevated over laity, the long acceptance of slavery among Christians, and the long oppression of women in the Christian church. Paul's vision has yet to be realized in its fullness.

---

1. The growth of hierarchy can represent an evolution in the functions of the church's ministry. Paul would probably accept that. But it often is accompanied by the establishment of a spiritual superiority system in the church. Paul would not accept that.

Despite the fact that we Christians keep drawing these distinctions of status in the church, Paul ends this section reminding his listeners of the critical point of his argument. All who belong to Christ are truly children of Abraham and therefore heirs of God's promise of blessing for those descendants. And the chief of those blessings is the gift of the Holy Spirit.

15

The New Era (Continued)

GALATIANS 4:1-11

[1] My point is this: heirs, as long as they are minors, are no better than slaves, though they are the owners of all the property; [2] but they remain under guardians and trustees until the date set by the father. [3] So with us; while we were minors, we were enslaved to the elemental spirits of the world. [4] But when the fullness of time had come, God sent his Son, born of a woman, born under the law, [5] in order to redeem those who were under the law, so that we might receive adoption as children. [6] And because you are children, God has sent the Spirit of his Son into our hearts, crying, "Abba! Father!" [7] So you are no longer a slave but a child, and if a child then also an heir, through God.

[8] Formerly, when you did not know God, you were enslaved to beings that by nature are not gods. [9] Now, however, that you have come to know God, or rather to be known by God, how can you turn back again to the weak and beggarly elemental spirits? How can you want to be enslaved to them again? [10] You are observing

special days, and months, and seasons, and years. [11] I am
afraid that my work for you may have been wasted.

SO FAR IN PAUL'S letter, we have heard his argument that Gentile
Christians do not need to conform their lives to the Jewish Torah.
Indeed, if they do, they are betraying the gospel. For Paul, the essence of the gospel is that we are justified (set in right relationship
with God) through faith in Christ or through the faith of Christ,
not by practice of the Jewish law.

The chapter division in our English Bibles do not represent
a distinct new move within Paul's argument. Rather, he continues
the argument that he has engaged in ever since verse 6 of chapter
1. In chapter 3, he developed a striking interpretation about the
role of the Jewish Torah. It was to be a kind of parental substitute
or disciplinarian that was to guide Israel until the Messiah came.

But once the Messiah came and brought in the kingdom of
God, Torah had served its purpose. No one needed any longer to
live by its demanding strictures, and certainly Gentile Christians
did not. In chapter 4 of his letter, Paul not only repeats this argument but also expands upon it.

In chapter 3 verses 15–18, Paul employs an analogy drawn
from daily life to explain his point. He appeals to the experience of
a person drawing up his or her last will and testament. Once someone has ratified that will, no one else can change it. Its provisions
are secure. In an analogous way, when God made the promises to
Abraham recorded in Genesis, we can rely on those promises as
secure because no one can change them except God and God is
faithful to his promises.

With the opening verses of chapter 4, Paul again turns to an
analogy drawn from ordinary, daily life to reinforce his argument.
But this time the analogy will not make much sense to us unless we
learn something about Greco-Roman family life, especially the le-
galities of family inheritance in a patrician Greek or Roman family.

In such a family, the father was the powerful ruler of the
household. In a traditional Roman family, in fact, the father was
the absolute ruler of the household. He literally held the power

of life and death over every member of that household, whether women, children, or slaves.

As long as the father's sons were minors, they differed little from slaves in the household. As boys, the sons did not have control of their lives. They had to obey their fathers—and the guardians that a father appointed over them—absolutely. In that respect, they differed little from slaves. One could even call their youth a kind of slavery.

When boys came of age—whatever that age was in different ethnic contexts—they became their own masters. They were no longer under their father's absolute rule. They could participate in civic life on the same level as other free citizens. That, however, was not the case with slaves. Slaves, regardless of their age, remained under the control of their masters all their lives.

Paul says that it is "so with us." We, too, were slaves to what the NRSV translates as the "elemental spirits of the world." What does he mean?

The Greek phrase the NRSV translates as "elemental spirits of the world" is *stoicheia tou cosmou*. Now, one thing that phrase can mean is the fundamental principles by which the pagan world understood life and the world. Today, we might call these the natural laws or abstract principles and processes of nature that science explores and reveals to us. They may also be the religious principles and practices by which pagan life governed itself.

On the other hand, *stoicheia tou cosmou* could refer to the gods that the pagans worshipped. Certainly in verse 8 below, Paul refers to these gods as beings who by nature are not really gods.

But there is a third option for interpretation. These *stoicheia tou cosmou* may also be the principles of religion espoused by the Jewish Torah.

How we interpret the phrase—and translate it into English— depends to a large degree on who Paul is referring to when he begins verse 3 with "so with us." If the *us* is Gentile Christians, then we are right to interpret the *stoicheia tou cosmou* as referring to the fundamental principles governing Gentile life, or the pagan gods.

If the *us* refers to Jewish Christians, then the *stoicheia tou cosmou* refers to the Jewish Torah. Paul is suggesting that Jews are slaves to the principles of their religion just as much as pagans are to theirs. That would be an alarming thing for Jewish Christians, especially the Judaizing teachers preaching in Galatia, to hear.

Biblical scholars debate which is the correct interpretation. Is it even an either-or interpretation? Is it possible that the ambiguity of Paul's expression is deliberate? Is he possibly suggesting that both pagans and Jews live under a shared slavery, even though their religious traditions are starkly different?

Whatever the meaning, Paul is saying the Galatian Christians, before their conversions, were living under some kind of religious slavery from which they have been set free. But if they start to order their lives by the strictures of Jewish Torah, says Paul, they are in effect returning to that kind of religious slavery from which they emerged, except in this case they would be adopting a slavery to Torah rather than a slavery to paganism. As Paul suggests in verse 10, a rigid observance of the Jewish calendar of religious festivals is, in principle, just another form of religious slavery.

Now let us return to the analogy of young boys coming of age. They enter into their status as free adults at that time that their father has appointed as the day of transition. In the Jewish, Greek, and Roman cultures, that time might come at a different age, but it would be accompanied by a special ceremony that initiated boys into their adult status.

That decisive moment of transition for the whole world has come in the specific historic time when Jesus was born, lived, died, rose again, and ascended into heaven. Paul calls that decisive event "the fullness of time."

It is the time when God sends his Son. Jesus is born as a human being (born of a woman) and as a Jew (born under the law). Whether Paul understands Jesus as preexisting in heaven before his birth, we cannot be sure. But Jesus's birth is no accident. He is "sent" by God.

His coming has a divine purpose. He is to redeem all who are in bondage so that they can become adopted sons of God. The language of redemption is the language of liberation. It looks back to the Old Testament practice of paying money to set an enslaved person, especially an enslaved member of the family, free. So the language of redemption is appropriate to the language of slavery and sonship that Paul is using.

Jesus redeems (liberates) by living out the Jewish Torah fully and faithfully, especially in accepting his unjust death as God's will for him. In so doing, Christ is the one true son of God and the one true son of Abraham to whom belong all the promises God made to Abraham and *his seed.*

All Christians join this family of God not by physical birth but by a spiritual adoption. They are adopted into God's family by their union with Christ through the act of faith that is expressed in baptism. Baptism then becomes a decisive point of transition in the life of each individual.

As adopted children of God, all Christians equally share with Christ in the promise of the inheritance. And as we saw in our discussion of chapter 3, Paul seems to understand the fulfillment of the promises made to Abraham as the gift of the Holy Spirit. This brings us back to the point Paul made at the beginning of chapter 3.

The Galatians have experienced the gift of the Holy Spirit. That shows that they are equally children of God with Christ. Under the inspiration of that Spirit, they call upon God as *Abba, Father.*

We will not understand why this is so important to Paul unless we pause to explore the significance of the word *Abba.* It is an Aramaic word that means *Father.* But in Aramaic it is a way of addressing one's father in an especially intimate way, for a literal translation would be *Daddy.*

We know from the gospels that *Abba* is the way Jesus himself addressed God. It was especially the way he called upon God in that anguished prayer in Gethsemane when Jesus struggled to accept his upcoming death as God's will for him (see Mark 14:36). Early Christians seemed to have picked up the practice of addressing God as *Abba* from Jesus's example.

For Paul, addressing God as *Abba* is preeminently the language of sonship. If Christians are doing so, then they are bearing witness that they are indeed children of God. And if they are children of God, then they are free children of God, not slaves. That entitles them to the inheritance of the kingdom of God when it comes in its fullness.

We take this analogy of status in the wrong way if we think that Christians become spiritually mature adults once they have been baptized. Paul is not saying any such thing, as he will make clearer in chapter 5, which will soon follow.

Instead, he makes the point that Christians share assurance that they will inherit the kingdom when it comes in the future. Christ has entered into that kingdom fully with his resurrection and ascension. We only experience in our Christian lives a foretaste of that coming kingdom as we experience life in the Holy Spirit.

So the reality is that we Christians live in a time between the times. God has liberated us from the various slaveries in which we live in this life, and yet we have not been set completely free as long as we live in our mortal bodies. However, because we have the gift of the Spirit, we can still begin to live as if we are in the kingdom, because in Christ we are. That paradox captures both the joy and the anguish of living the Christian life.

16

A Deeply Personal Appeal

GALATIANS 4:12-20

[12] Friends, I beg you, become as I am, for I also have become as you are. You have done me no wrong. [13] You know that it was because of a physical infirmity that I first announced the gospel to you; [14] though my condition put you to the test, you did not scorn or despise me, but welcomed me as an angel of God, as Christ Jesus. [15] What has become of the good will you felt? For I testify that, had it been possible, you would have torn out your eyes and given them to me. [16] Have I now become your enemy by telling you the truth? [17] They make much of you, but for no good purpose; they want to exclude you, so that you may make much of them. [18] It is good to be made much of for a good purpose at all times, and not only when I am present with you. [19] My little children, for whom I am again in the pain of childbirth until Christ is formed in you, [20] I wish I were present with you now and could change my tone, for I am perplexed about you.

IF WE HAVE BEEN paying close attention to what Paul has said in the letter so far, we will have noted how skilled Paul is as a debater. He has employed a number of approaches to his argumentation. In chapters 1 and 2, he defends the gospel he preaches by defending his apostolic commission. He tells us the story of his own conversion and his experience of God sending him out to preach the gospel to Gentiles. He also shows how the apostles in Jerusalem, Jesus's original disciples, recognized his commission.

In 3:1–5, Paul makes an appeal to the Galatians' own experience of conversion. He reminds them of their very real experience of the Holy Spirit working in their midst. Rhetorically, this is an explicit appeal to religious experience.

In 3:6–14, he appeals to Scripture, the Old Testament. His argument draws upon the style of rabbinic exegesis that he was trained in as a young man. Through it he draws a startling conclusion, for a Jew at least. Because of the coming of Christ, now Gentiles as well as Jews belong to the family of Abraham and share in the blessing God has promised to Abraham and his descendants.

In 3:15—4:10, Paul turns to analogies drawn from the daily life of Gentiles in the Greco-Roman world to clarify the role of the Jewish Torah in God's plan. It was to serve a temporary role until the Messiah came. Now its job is complete. Both Gentile and Jew are called from their respective religious cultures into a new freedom that comes in Christ.

In these various arguments, we see the astonishing creativity of Paul in developing his case. With 4:11–20, Paul will now turn to a new appeal. But it will be different from the others. The other arguments have been largely rational in character. In some cases, as with the appeal to Scripture, the argument has been complex. We have to pay very close attention to what Paul is saying and to the sources on which he is drawing.

This new appeal, however, has a distinctly emotional and personal character. Paul appeals to the Galatians' experience with him during the time he was evangelizing them. The thought jumps around a bit, as do our thoughts when they are expressive of our emotions rather than of our organized rational thinking.

Paul begins by asking the Galatians to imitate him. He is not setting up himself as some paragon of ethical virtue. If he were, he would not ask them to imitate him but to imitate Christ. Rather he wants them to imitate him in this issue of living by the Jewish Torah.

As a Jew, he grew up under Torah. As a young adult, he was zealous in defending Torah and all the Jewish way of life that it defined. But after his encounter with Christ, he came to see Torah as subordinate to Christ. In his new zeal to bring the gospel to Gentiles, he has come to live like a Gentile, abandoning conformity to the Jewish Torah. The Galatians are being tempted to take on the yoke of Torah. Instead, he wants them to put that yoke aside as he has since his conversion. He exhorts them to live out the gospel he has been preaching all along.

He then reminds them of their first experiences with him when he arrived in Galatia and started preaching the gospel to them. Here he is asking them to look back and remember their own conversions.

He says he first preached the gospel in Galatia as a result of a serious illness. We can't really say what this illness was. Scholars have offered a number of speculations: an eye disease, malaria, epilepsy, or maybe serious injuries from some form of public flogging. We simply don't know.

But whatever it was, it seems to have been a condition that would normally repel people. In verse 14, when he says that they did not despise him, the NRSV translates a Greek verb that literally means "spit upon." Now, Paul may mean this metaphorically, but Greeks regarded some diseases as an expression of demon possession. They felt it was appropriate, therefore, to literally spit on the sick person. If Paul has this idea of demon possession in mind, then when he talks of them receiving him as an angel, the contrast would be especially vivid. Indeed, they had received him as if he were Christ himself.

They had indeed received and welcomed him with warmth and compassion. After all this, he asks, how could they now regard him as an enemy? He can only conclude that the Judaizing teachers working among them have maligned his reputation and motives. In response, he questions theirs. He charges that they are zealously working among the Galatians for their own egotistic motives and that they want to exclude the Galatians outside the community of faith, so that the Galatians will come seeking them. This will build up their reputation within the Christian community, especially in the important Jewish Christian community in Jerusalem.

In verse 19, we find one of Paul's most surprising analogies. He compares evangelism and pastoral care to a kind of spiritual pregnancy. Like a mother bearing her child in her womb, the apostle experiences pain and anguish in carrying these embryo Christians as Christ is being formed in them.

This verse gives us an insight into the anxiety that pastoral care brought into Paul's life. He so loves these new communities of faith in Galatia that he experiences deep anxiety over their welfare. Will they grow up into mature communities of faith? Will their lives be so transformed that they will image out Christ to their world?

We get another glimpse of the anxiety Paul feels as a pastor in a passage found in 2 Corinthians 11:21–28. There, too, Paul is facing the charge that he is not a very effective apostle, like the super-apostles that the Corinthian believers seem to revere. Paul then begins a list of the various trials and sufferings he has endured in his ministry. They include beatings, imprisonments, shipwrecks, danger from bandits, sleepless nights, and hunger.

The last thing he lists (in verse 28) is his "anxiety for all the churches." Coming at the end of the list, this item holds the position of rhetorical importance, suggesting that Paul regards it as the greatest of his many trials and tribulations. For Paul, true pastoral care is no life of calm labor and leisure. It is filled with anxiety as the pastor yearns to see his congregation grow into a mature community of faith. Many a pastor today could affirm Paul's description of the pastoral experience.

Paul fears, however, that the spiritual pregnancy he had begun with them is turning into a miscarriage. If they opt to go the way of the Judaizing teachers, then they may prove to be still born. Thought of that gives him deep anguish. We get another insight into this anguish when he calls the Galatians "my little children" in verse 19. In Greek, the words "little children" are in a diminutive form. In a more colloquial translation, we might translate them "my little kiddies."

The words strike a note of a very tender affection. The Galatians may regard Paul now as an enemy, but Paul does not so regard them. They are his spiritual children, and he continues to love them and adore them.

This is a very needed emotional note in the letter at this point. Paul has written some very sharp rebukes. More will come. But the Galatians need to understand that his words of rebuke are motivated not by hostility but by deep parental love.

It is also a very wise pastoral move. It is sometimes said that no pastor earns the right to preach judgment and rebuke to his or her congregation until he or she has first established a deep level of trust and assurance of his or her love for the congregation. Otherwise the congregation will take the words of judgment and rebuke as expressions of rejection rather than of compassion.

17

Another Appeal to Scripture

²¹ Tell me, you who desire to be subject to the law, will you not listen to the law? ²² For it is written that Abraham had two sons, one by a slave woman and the other by a free woman. ²³ One, the child of the slave, was born according to the flesh; the other, the child of the free woman, was born through the promise. ²⁴ Now this is an allegory: these women are two covenants. One woman, in fact, is Hagar, from Mount Sinai, bearing children for slavery. ²⁵ Now Hagar is Mount Sinai in Arabia and corresponds to the present Jerusalem, for she is in slavery with her children. ²⁶ But the other woman corresponds to the Jerusalem above; she is free, and she is our mother. ²⁷ For it is written,

> "Rejoice, you childless one, you who bear no children,
>   burst into song and shout, you who endure no
>   birth pangs;
> for the children of the desolate woman are more
>   numerous
> than the children of the one who is married."

²⁸ Now you, my friends, are children of the promise, like Isaac. ²⁹ But just as at that time the child who was born according to the flesh persecuted the child who was born according to the Spirit, so it is now also. ³⁰ But what does the scripture say? "Drive out the slave and her child; for the child of the slave will not share the inheritance with the child of the free woman." ³¹ So then, friends, we are children, not of the slave but of the free woman.

AFTER HIS DEEPLY PERSONAL appeal to those who would have heard this letter read aloud to them in their worship gathering, Paul returns once again to an appeal to Scripture. He does so as he works his argument up to a climax. That climax is the action he wants the Galatian Christians to do. It will be suggested through a quotation from the Old Testament.

In chapter 3, we watched Paul as he interpreted Scripture in the pattern of the Jewish rabbis of his day. Paul had been trained well. He could match them in skill.

In this passage, however, Paul demonstrates his skill in interpreting Scripture in an alternative way of exegesis. This time, rather than using the ways of detailed word and grammatical analysis, ways preferred by Palestinian rabbis, he interprets Scripture like a Greek literary scholar.

The Greeks regarded texts like Homer's *Iliad* and *Odyssey* as well as some of the traditional myths as the core texts of Greek education. They used them to teach young people fundamental moral and philosophical principles.

But how do you draw moral instruction out of these narratives, especially given the capricious and salacious ways often practiced by the Greek gods? Greek educators did this by interpreting the texts allegorically. They regarded details in the narratives as symbols disclosing philosophical truths or moral principles.

This style of literary interpretation was especially popular among Greek literary scholars working in the Greek city of Alexandria, Egypt. The city had its famous library, which served as a center of literary scholarship.

It seems that it was in Alexandria that Jewish scholars were exposed to this style of literary interpretation. One Jewish scholar in particular excelled in it. He was Philo, who was a contemporary of Paul. A large selection of Philo's works has survived, and in them he uses this Greek style of allegory to interpret the Jewish Scriptures and make them relevant to Jews living in a Greek intellectual culture.

Later Christian scholars in the city also picked up this style of Scriptural interpretation. They left behind a model of allegorical interpretation that was to be very popular and influential through the Middle Ages.

When Paul returns to his argument by this new appeal to Scripture, he will work with Scripture in this distinctly Greek way. It is possible that this would have spoken forcefully to those Gentile Galatians to whom he was writing. As Greek speakers, they may have felt very at home with this style of literary interpretation.

When Paul returns to the Old Testament, he returns again to the story of Abraham in Genesis. This time, his focus will be on two chapters in Genesis, 16 and 21. Although Abraham's wife Sarah was barren, God had promised that Abraham would have a son. The fulfillment of the promise, however, was slow. As a result, Sarah suggests that Abraham father a child through her Egyptian slave girl Hagar. Hagar conceives and bears a son, who is named Ishmael. The conception comes through normal sexual relations. This story is told in Genesis 16.

Later, as a result of God's miraculous intervention, Sarah, too, conceives and bears a son even though she is way past child-bearing age. The child is named Isaac. He is the child of God's promise.

As the children grow up together, Sarah finds Ishmael one day apparently mocking Isaac. That is at least how many rabbis read the text of Genesis 21:9. So Sarah demands that Abraham drive Hagar and her son out of the family. She does so in the words of Genesis 21:10, saying, "Cast out this slave woman with her son; for the son of this slave woman shall not inherit along with my son Isaac."

Using the technique of allegorical interpretation, Paul identifies Hagar and Ishmael with the Sinai covenant that God established with the Jews through Moses. Its stipulations are expressed in the Torah, which regulates Jewish life. Earlier in chapters 3 and 4, Paul has already characterized life under Torah as a kind of slavery, parallel to Greek slavery to the elemental principles of Greek religion. So he easily makes Hagar and Ishmael symbols of a Christian life lived under Torah.

But notice he identifies the Gentile Christians in Galatia with Sarah and Isaac. From this identification he draws the conclusion in verse 28, "Now you, my friends, are children of the promise, like Isaac." They do not need to adopt the stipulations of Torah.

From this he then comes to the action he wants them to take. Just as Sarah demanded that Abraham cast out Hagar and her son, these Galatian Christians need to drive out the Judaizing teachers who are troubling their life as a church.

Now these eleven verses are a tricky passage for modern Christians today to read and absorb. For one thing, most biblical scholars today do not favor an allegorical interpretation of Scripture. Allegory was a popular form of literature during the Middle Ages and into some early eras of modern times. One thinks of masterpieces like Dante's *Divine Comedy* and John Bunyan's *Pilgrim's Progress*.

But Protestant Reformers like Martin Luther, John Calvin, and others tended to frown on the allegorical reading of the Bible. It opened doors for all kinds of irresponsible readings of the texts. One could use allegory to inject one's personal whims into the text and then give those whims the authority of Holy Scripture.

Allegory is sometimes used in other parts of the New Testament. A familiar example is the interpretation that Jesus gives to his parable of the sower as recorded in Mark 4:1–9, 14–20 (and in parallel passages in Matt 13 and Luke 8). But today, we often find such a way of interpreting Scripture unconvincing.

It is important, then, that in reading this passage in Galatians we keep in mind the action that Paul is using this allegory to urge his listeners to take. They are to cast out the Judaizing teachers who are troubling them. The allegory becomes a tool as Paul drives to that action.

Second, we today are going to be very uncomfortable with the implied judgment Paul seems to be making upon the religion of Judaism in this passage. When in verse 24 Paul talks about two covenants, we are entering into the conceptual world where Christians see Judaism as the old covenant (in Latin the Old Testament) and Christianity as the new covenant (New Testament).

From this distinction, it is easy to move on to see Judaism not only as the old covenant, but also as the discarded or displaced covenant. Once we make that step, we have stepped into the pathway that will lead to the whole ugly history of Christian anti-Semitism.

Is there anything then we can do with this passage (Gal 4:21–31) besides wishing that Paul had never written it? Let me make a couple of suggestions.

First, let us keep in mind that Paul's opponents in Galatia were not traditional Jews, but Jewish Christians, or Gentile Christians, who advocated that all Gentile Christians should adopt and live by the Jewish Torah. He is not advocating that the Galatian Christians drive all Jews out of Galatia. He is advocating instead they drive out the Judaizing Christian teachers who are troubling their congregational life.

That is to make a very subtle distinction, I admit. But we must keep that distinction clearly in mind lest we read this text as legitimizing anti-Semitism.

The other thing I would say is that we keep in mind that Paul, throughout this letter, keeps pushing our attention back past the Sinai narrative to the even earlier narrative of Abraham in Genesis. Even there he pushes us back past the institution of circumcision in Genesis 17 to the call of Abraham in Genesis 12 and the establishment of the covenant between God and Abraham in Genesis 15.

Why is that? I would like to suggest that Paul wants to clearly call our attention to the fact that Judaism and Christianity, at their very central core, are *both* religions of grace. God takes the initiative to reach out and establish a relationship with both Jews and

Christians *first* before any regulations are laid upon either group. As I indicated in my discussion of the Exodus experience in my second theological reflection, liberation from Egypt comes before the giving of the Torah at Mount Sinai, just as liberation from sin and death through Christ comes before any obedient action by Christians.

That God's liberating action has consequences for the way we live, whether we are Jews or Christians, is the other side of the message of grace. It is the message of the Torah given at Sinai. It will be Paul's message as well as we enter next into chapters 5 and 6 of Galatians. But our behavior does not earn us God's grace. It is the consequence of God's grace.

But when Jewish understandings of Torah displace this message of grace, and when Christian tradition equally with its mandated doctrines, ethics, and liturgical practices displaces grace, then both religions easily fall back into the religious bondage that Paul identifies in his discussion. We see this fall into bondage throughout Christian churches today wherever specified doctrines, behaviors, and attitudes become the defining criteria as to who is Christian and who is not.

So when we Christians today read Paul's distinction between Hagar and her son and Sarah and her son, we need to soberly ask: On which side of that distinction do we fall into today?

18

Theological Reflection
Christians: Who Are They?

IF I WERE TO summarize the Pauline understanding of the Christian life, I would do so in the two words Paul uses over and over again in Galatians: *in Christ*, or in Greek, *en Christo*. When he talks about Christians, he describes them as being *in Christ*.

I have highlighted the phrase in italics in these examples to make the point:

> But because of false believers secretly brought in, who slipped in to spy on the freedom we have *in Christ Jesus*, so that they might enslave us. (Gal 2:4)

> But if, in our effort to be justified *in Christ*, we ourselves have been found to be sinners, is Christ then a servant of sin? (Gal 2:17)

> That *in Christ Jesus* the blessing of Abraham might come to the Gentiles, so that we might receive the promise of the Spirit through faith. (Gal 3:14)

> For *in Christ Jesus* you are all children of God through faith. (Gal 3:26)

There is no longer Jew or Greek, there is no longer slave or free, there is no longer male and female; for all of you are one *in Christ Jesus*. (Gal 3:28)

For *in Christ Jesus* neither circumcision nor uncircumcision counts for anything; the only thing that counts is faith working through love. (Gal 5:6)

For anyone raised from childhood in a church, the phrase will sound so familiar as to be almost unnoticed. But that means we are likely to overlook its strangeness. We expect Paul to talk about Christians as *of Christ*, in the sense of belonging to Christ as disciples following a teacher. But instead Paul talks about Christians being *in Christ*. In this peculiar wording we glimpse something profound in Paul's theological vision.

LIVING THE CHRISTIAN LIFE IN CHRIST

In Paul's vision, we as Christians are justified, saved, and redeemed, not simply *by* Christ, but *in* Christ. What redeems us is the faith *of* Christ. His faithfulness is the key to our salvation. This comes through in two crucial passages in the letter:

We ourselves are Jews by birth and not Gentile sinners; yet we know that a person is justified not by the works of the law but through faith in Jesus Christ [Greek: *pistis Jesou Christou*]. And we have come to believe in Christ Jesus, so that we might be justified by faith in Christ [*pistis Christou*], and not by doing the works of the law, because no one will be justified by the works of the law. (Gal 2:15–16)

But the scripture has imprisoned all things under the power of sin, so that what was promised through faith in Jesus Christ [*pistis Jesou Christou*] might be given to those who believe. (Gal 3:22)

We saw earlier how in these two verses the Greek phrase *pistis Christou* can carry two meanings and two translations. It can mean "faith in Christ" or "the faith of Christ."

My understanding of Paul is that he says what redeems us is the faith (or faithfulness) *of* Christ. The faith of Christ is Jesus's life of perfect faith, a trust in God that extends even to accepting God's will of an ignominious death as a supposed criminal on a cross. The cross is not an unfortunate and preventable accident, but part of God's will for Jesus. This life of faith perfectly fulfills the Old Testament Torah. As a result, God raises Jesus from the dead to eternal life and bestows the full gift of the Holy Spirit, which Paul sees as the fulfillment of the promise made to Abraham (Gal 3:14). And it is the Spirit which gives life to us.

How do Christians receive the Holy Spirit? Paul says we receive the Holy Spirit *in* Christ. We must be united with Christ in a profoundly spiritual way. As a result of this union between Christ and believers, a profound transformation takes place in the life of the believer.

Here is where we must pay close attention to what Paul says in Galatians 2:19–20:

> For through the law I died to the law, so that I might live to God. I have been crucified with Christ; and it is no longer I who live, but it is Christ who lives in me. And the life I now live in the flesh I live by faith in the Son of God, who loved me and gave himself for me.

Notice carefully how Paul describes his life as a Christian: Christ lives *in* me and I *in* Christ. Something profound has taken place in Paul's own life, and it proves the key to his understanding of what God is doing in Jesus Christ.

Scholars sometimes label this aspect of Paul's theology as Paul's Christ mysticism. It dramatically transforms his thinking on the dynamics of Christian behavior, as we will see in a later discussion.

UNITED WITH CHRIST IN THE ACTION OF BAPTISM

How are we united with Christ? In Galatians 2:16–20, we find this union is accomplished by faith, but it also involves a kind of dying and being raised again. Our faith in Christ expresses itself in the *action* of baptism, which, as Paul will be explicit about in Romans 6:3–4, involves an experience of dying and being resurrected.

In baptism we *put on* Christ, like a garment (Gal 3:27). As we saw, the language in this verse may be an allusion to the new baptismal robe that the newly baptized put on after their immersion into the baptismal waters. Paul's language, however, also seems to bear witness to a deeply spiritual experience for the newly baptized. In baptism, the new converts experience something more than a symbolic rite. They undergo a profoundly transforming spiritual experience.

In Galatians 3:26, Paul speaks of Christians becoming adopted children of God *in* Christ. And in Galatians 3:29, he says we receive *in* Christ the blessing which was promised to Abraham's descendants, the gift of the Holy Spirit.

Baptism is also the entrance rite into the community of the church. We come to be in Christ by our entrance into the church. It is in the church where the Holy Spirit is at work to transform human beings. The church and Christ are one, because the church is the body of Christ in the world.

This, I believe, is one of the major insights Paul received from his Damascus Road experience. Paul does not discuss this in Galatians, but he does in his other epistles, especially 1 Corinthians. Life in Christ is fundamentally a communal life, a life lived in a community with other believers. We may be saved at the Last Judgment by an individual faith in Christ, but we stunt our Christian growth if we do not unite ourselves with other believers in a Christian community.

WHO THEN IS A CHRISTIAN?

Paul's vision of the Christian life as being *in Christ* answers the question: Who is a Christian? A Christian is someone who has united himself or herself with Christ by faith *in* Christ and Christ's saving action on our behalf.

Paul's answer has profound consequences for how we determine who is a Christian today.

Some define a Christian by his or her spiritual experience. They will say you *must* be born again, meaning you have to have a strikingly emotional conversion experience.[1] Others might say you *must* speak in tongues.

Some will define a Christian by his or her beliefs. You *must* believe in the Apostles' Creed or the Nicene Creed or some other authoritative statement of the content of Christian belief.

Some will define a Christian by the ethical or social stances he or she takes on important issues of contention. They will say you *must* adopt certain stances in the world, such as opposition to abortion or homosexuality, or you *must* be active in serving the poor and disadvantaged. Or you must be a pacifist.

And from the language we sometimes hear in political discourse, some seem to define a Christian by his or her political allegiance. You *must* be a Republican or a Democrat.

Note how in each of these stances I have highlighted the word *must*. Here is where the language of the Judaizing teachers in Galatia can begin to take on a contemporary ring. They, too, were speaking the language of *must*. In their case, they were trying to define the Christian by the *must* of observing Torah.

1. I acknowledge that Jesus himself uses the word *must* in John 3:7, when he says to Nicodemus, "You must be born again [or "from above"]." One must be born from above, he says, to enter into the Kingdom of God. I agree with that. What I am contesting is the tendency in some Christian circles to identify being *born again* with one particular kind of conversion experience, especially the kind of altar-call conversion experience so favored by the revivalist tradition in America. Jesus says we must be born from above. He does not say, however, just how that happens in terms of a particular evangelistic technique or emotional experience. If Jesus does not get specific on the how, then I think Christians need to be reticent on defining the how as well.

Paul vehemently rejects the stance that you *must* be circumcised and live by Jewish customs to be a Christian. I believe he would just as vehemently reject the other musts we hear in the contemporary Christian world. Anytime we hear a preacher or other Christians using the word *must* to describe something Christians do or believe, we need to be on guard. For Paul, what makes someone a Christian is faith *in* Jesus Christ, period.

When I am asked how I define a Christian, I like to refer to an expression one American church denomination has used to define church membership. It reads this way:

> The Church universal consists of all persons in every nation, together with their children, who profess faith in Jesus Christ as Lord and Savior and commit themselves to live in a fellowship under his rule.[2]

I find this a very Pauline definition of church membership. It identifies a Christian by two features:

1. A profession of faith in Jesus Christ as Lord and Savior. Notice that the language talks about a profession of faith. It does not seek to determine the genuineness of any person's religious experience. Only God can judge that. But one can hear and accept a profession of faith.

2. A commitment to living in a fellowship under Christ's rule. This involves a commitment to living in a community of fellow believers under the lordship of Christ. Normally that fellowship will prove to be a local congregation of the church.

This means Catholics are Christians, Quakers are Christians, Baptists are Christians, Pentecostals are Christians, Methodists are Christians, Presbyterians are Christians, Lutherans are Christians, Eastern Orthodox are Christians, and Egyptian Copts are Christians if we profess faith in Jesus Christ as Lord and Savior and commit to live in a fellowship under Christ's rule.

---

2. This statement on church membership was found in versions of the *Book of Order: The Constitution of the Presbyterian Church (USA)* before 2011. See Paragraph G-4.0101. It was dropped from a revision adopted in that year.

LEGITIMATE DIVERSITY WITHIN THE CHRISTIAN MOVEMENT

This way of defining a Christian then has a corollary. It means no one theology, liturgy, ethical formulation, or church polity is *the one and only* Christian position. We are faced with the reality that there can be a great diversity of theologies, liturgies, ethical formulations, and polities in the church. Not all may be equally faithful, but all can be Christian. Diversity is not necessarily a sign of apostasy.

For Paul, that diversity also implies a radical equality within the church. There are no first- and second-class citizens in the church. There is no place for a spiritual elite in the church. Here is where we glimpse the critical importance of Galatians 3:27–28 for Paul's vision:

> For as many of you as were baptized into Christ have put on Christ. There is neither Jew nor Greek, there is neither slave nor free, there is neither male nor female; for you are all one in Christ Jesus.

Christianity has compromised on Paul's vision throughout church history, but we need to recognize our compromises as a departure from the high vision articulated by Paul.

19

Stand Firm in Your Freedom

GALATIANS 5:1

> [1] For freedom Christ has set us free. Stand firm, there-
> fore, and do not submit again to a yoke of slavery.

ANCIENT MANUSCRIPTS, INCLUDING THOSE of the Bible, were written without paragraph breaks, word divisions, or punctuation. A
text ran on in one continuous line. So when we today divide the
text into paragraphs (to make it easier to read), we sometimes have
to make sensitive decisions where one paragraph ends and another
begins.

We face one such decision when we come to Galatians 5:1.
Does this verse form the conclusion of Galatians 4:21–31? That is
the conclusion that the translators of the NRSV made. They make
it the last sentence of the paragraph. Many other versions of the
Bible do the same.

The translators of the Revised Standard Version and of the
New International Version make the exact opposite conclusion.
They regard the verse as the opening of a brand new section.

What these contrasting decisions do is highlight how this verse functions both as a bridge between two blocks of discussion in the letter and as a definitive conclusion to Paul's theological argument.

As a conclusion to Paul's argument, the verse states in a nutshell the bottom line of Paul's theological argument in chapters 1–4. What God has accomplished through Christ is an act of spiritual liberation. The Galatian Gentile Christians must not compromise that liberation by any adoption of the traditions of Jewish Torah as a requirement for their Christian faithfulness. If they have not fully followed all the twists and turns of his theological argument, they can hold on to this simple conclusion.

The verse also serves as a bridge. It makes the transition between the first four chapters of the letter and its final two. In those first four chapters Paul makes his theological argument. Now he will turn to the practical implications that his theology has for the way the Galatian Christians need to live. We might summarize this as a transition from theology proper to what I rather loosely call ethics and spirituality.

The pivot on which that transition swings is the word *therefore*. The theology is that Christ has set us free. The behavioral outcome of that theology is that we now need to stand firm in our freedom. We must not return to slavery. We make that transition through the word *therefore*.

This is a characteristic feature of Paul's letters. They generally follow this same pattern. The first part of the letter lays out Paul's theological points. It is what God has accomplished for us through the death and resurrection of Christ. The second part of the letter spells out what implications God's action has for the way we are now to live.

The pivot point over and over again is the word *therefore*. Biblical scholars label it the Pauline Therefore. We see the finest example of this style in Paul's Letter to the Romans. In chapters 1–11, Paul expounds his theology. With chapter 12, he moves to how this theology should influence how we live. He does so with these inspiring words:

> I appeal to you therefore, brothers and sisters, by the mercies of God, to present your bodies as a living sacrifice, holy and acceptable to God, which is your spiritual worship. Do not be conformed to this world, but be transformed by the renewing of your minds, so that you may discern what is the will of God—what is good and acceptable and perfect. (Rom 12:1–2)

The same pivot happens in Galatians 5:1.

There is a second pivot also going on in this verse, although we don't realize it until we read further into chapter 5. Paul is talking all about freedom, but what does he mean by the word freedom? He does not mean license to do whatever we please, license to follow every whim we experience. Nor does it mean license to live a totally self-centered life in which all that counts is the welfare of me and my own.

What Paul means by freedom will become clearer as we move deeper into this new chapter.

20

What Really Counts

GALATIANS 5:2–12

² Listen! I, Paul, am telling you that if you let yourselves be circumcised, Christ will be of no benefit to you. ³ Once again I testify to every man who lets himself be circumcised that he is obliged to obey the entire law. ⁴ You who want to be justified by the law have cut yourselves off from Christ; you have fallen away from grace. ⁵ For through the Spirit, by faith, we eagerly wait for the hope of righteousness. ⁶ For in Christ Jesus neither circumcision nor uncircumcision counts for anything; the only thing that counts is faith working through love.

⁷ You were running well; who prevented you from obeying the truth? ⁸ Such persuasion does not come from the one who calls you. ⁹ A little yeast leavens the whole batch of dough. ¹⁰ I am confident about you in the Lord that you will not think otherwise. But whoever it is that is confusing you will pay the penalty. ¹¹ But my friends, why am I still being persecuted if I am still preaching circumcision? In that case the offense of the cross has

been removed. [12] I wish those who unsettle you would castrate themselves!

IN THE PREVIOUS SECTION, I described Galatians 5:1 as the turning point in the letter. At this point Paul will move from his theological discussion to a discussion of Christian behavior. On one level, that is accurate. On another, it is not. Because before Paul fully launches into issues of behavior, he will once more underscore the dividing issue between himself and the Judaizing teachers troubling the churches in Galatia. He wants us to have that difference clearly in mind, and to ensure that we do, he will use some of the most forceful, indeed sometimes shocking, language he has yet used in the letter.

There can be no compromise in the debate between Paul and the Judaizing party. It is either the Torah or Christ. Which is Lord?

For Paul, if the Galatians accept the argument of the Judaizers and undergo circumcision, then they apostatize. They will fall from grace. They will sever their bond with Christ. In today's terms, we might say that they will cease to be Christians.

To say the least, this is strong, passionate language. What lies behind it? One hint is contained in verse 3. If any man lets himself be circumcised, Paul says, he does not just adopt a quaint ritual practice that allows him to earn acceptance in a Jewish community. He is, in fact, taking the first step that will obligate him to live his whole life by the stipulations of the Jewish Torah.

The Judaizing teachers may have suggested that Paul had not preached the necessity of circumcision to his Galatian converts in an effort to make the gospel more palatable to Gentiles. Paul turns the tables on this argument. His language hints that they are the ones who are accommodating to Gentile sensibilities.

It is possible the Judaizers were suggesting that if Gentile Christians just accepted circumcision, that is all they would need to do to placate the sensitivities of their Jewish brothers. If that were the case, Paul is saying that the Galatians are being deceived. If you adopt circumcision, you are obligating yourself to live by all the commandments of Torah. You cannot pick and choose which you will adopt and which you will reject. And if you live totally by Torah, then you are in fact a Jew, not a Gentile Christian.

In this argument, Paul appeals to the Galatians' self-interest. If you accept circumcision, you put your salvation in jeopardy. Is that what you really want?

In verse 6 we get the statement of a theological principle that equals Galatians 5:1 in its timeless truth. In Christ, he says, neither circumcision nor uncircumcision count for anything. All that counts is faith working through love. This is a summary of Paul's understanding of the Christian life in a nutshell.

Let us unpack it to better understand what Paul is saying. We have seen already that when Paul talks of faith, what he has in mind is not belief in certain propositional truths. Yes, the gospel declares certain truths about what God has accomplished, is accomplishing, and will accomplish through Jesus Christ. It makes declarations about the death and resurrection of Jesus that we are invited to believe.

Believing those proclamations, however, is not what Paul means by faith. They set the stage for faith. If we believe these proclamations, we are then invited to put our trust in this God who is at work in Jesus, to place our personal confidence in this God and his promises. And we live our lives according to that trust that we place in God. Faith becomes, therefore, something that involves our thinking, our feelings, and our behavior.

This faith, this confidence in God, expresses itself in our way of living. Faith and works are not at odds with each other. Rather they are the two sides of this relationship we have with God. It is hard to call it faith unless we are expressing that faith in the way we live. This is the idea expressed in the translator's phrasing "working through."

Finally, for Paul, the critical expression of faith in behavior is behavior that expresses love. The faithful behavior that the gospel calls us to is not rote observance of laws and ethical principles. Those laws and principles point toward what faithful behavior looks like, which is the living out of love. This love is not just warm and pious feelings for God or for other people. It is concrete action in which we work for the good of others. For Paul, Christian love (*agape*) is always more about action than about feelings.

In this phrase, faith expresses the vertical dimension of our Christian lives. It places our trust and confidence in God. Love expresses the horizontal dimension. It behaves in ways that work for the good and well-being of others, even, as Jesus makes clear in the Sermon on the Mount, for the well-being of our enemies. What Paul says takes only four words to say, but what depth those four words contain!

With verse 7, Paul returns to the exasperation he feels over what the Galatian Christians are contemplating doing. "You were running well," he says. This metaphor compares their Christian spiritual journey to a Greek foot race. Who then interfered with your running? Who sidetracked you? It was not I, says Paul.

If the Galatians are inclined to look upon the issue of circumcision as a minor issue in the life of the church, then they are badly mistaken, says Paul. It poses a serious danger. To make clear how serious, he compares the issue to the effect yeast has in bread dough. Just a small amount of yeast makes the whole dough rise.

Yeast was a common Jewish image for the power of evil. The bread served at Passover was always unleavened bread. In preparation for Passover, Jewish women seek to remove all yeast from the household. Yeast remains a metaphor for how a little bit of evil can end up corrupting the whole spiritual community. The unexpressed conclusion is that the Galatian churches should cast out these Judaizing teachers from their fellowship, just as Jewish wives would rid their house of yeast at Passover. If they do not, they run the risk of these teachers corrupting their whole community life.

That these teachers are hostile toward Paul is clear from what Paul alludes to in verse 11. He mentions how he is being persecuted for his stance. Paul returns the hostility in the next verse, where he expresses the wish that those who unsettle the Galatians with their demand that Gentile male believers be circumcised would not only cut off their own foreskins, but then go on to castrate themselves.

To my sensibilities, this is one of the most shocking things that Paul writes in any of his letters. He may be engaging in some crude humor or in some deep sarcasm. He may also be alluding to the Torah principle that eunuchs are not permitted to participate in the temple's worship (see Deut 23:1). Or we may just be witnessing the depth of exasperation Paul feels over the whole controversy. But whatever Paul's intention, I find his language crude and rude. Here Paul is no paragon of moderation. And one wonders if Paul has not set a very unfortunate example for the rest of Christian history. In church controversy after church controversy, Christians have repeatedly engaged in bitter name-calling and personal insults. The Reformation era, for example, provides an abundance of examples, both by Catholics and Protestants.

Those who engage in such practices can appeal to the example of the Apostle Paul. If the apostle had known how his own words set such a tragic example for others to follow after him, I sometimes wonder if he would have been more circumspect in what he said.

Issues of great moment have been at stake in many church controversies, but does that fact give sanction for the bitterness and downright meanness that many Christians have shown toward their doctrinal or ecclesiastical opponents within the family of faith? For myself, I do not believe it does. I believe we can disagree vigorously with each other and still be civil toward each other. But many will see it otherwise.

21

Responsible Freedom

GALATIANS 5:13-15

> [13] For you were called to freedom, brothers and sisters;
> only do not use your freedom as an opportunity for
> self-indulgence, but through love become slaves to one
> another. [14] For the whole law is summed up in a single
> commandment, "You shall love your neighbor as your-
> self." [15] If, however, you bite and devour one another, take
> care that you are not consumed by one another.

WITH VERSE 13, PAUL finally turns to the issues of Christian behavior. What is the kind of behavior that expresses the freedom
that Christ has conferred upon the Galatians? What is the kind of
freedom, we ask, that Christ has conferred upon us?

Before he launches into the specifics of behavior, Paul seems
to want to make sure that his listeners do not misunderstand what
he has to say about the freedom of the Gentile Christians. Freedom, after all, can mean many different things to different people,
to different cultures, and to different ideologies. It was a very po-
tent word within Greek culture, which prized the ideal of freedom.

What Paul makes immediately clear as he speaks in verse 13 is that by the word *freedom* he does not mean personal autonomy. That kind of freedom means a person is free to choose to do whatever his or her whims motivate him or her to do. Freedom as personal independence tends to express itself in behavior that strives for power or status, for one's own personal well-being, especially as that well-being is defined by the culture in which one lives. For Paul, this kind of freedom is inherently egocentric.

Rather, the freedom that Christ confers upon us by his redemptive death and resurrection is a liberation from this domineering egocentrism, which fuels sin. By offering the possibility of being set free from this domination, Christ removes the barriers that block us from living out the life that God calls us to. We are being called to a responsible freedom.

This freedom that Christ confers involves a paradox. It frees us from the tyranny of sin and egocentrism so that we can become the slave serving others under the lordship of Christ. We are not given personal autonomy. Rather, we exchange one lord for another. Yet when we acknowledge and live under the lordship of Christ, we find our service brings not a diminishment of life, but an enrichment. Christ's lordship is a lordship that aims not at his own egocentric power and glory, but at the well-being and fulfillment of those who serve him.

This new slavery, a mutual servanthood of love, also fulfills the very purpose and momentum of the Jewish Torah. That Torah is summed up, says Paul, in the admonition to love your neighbor as yourself. If we live by this principle, we build up a wholesome community life in which all flourish. For Paul, the supreme good is not the well-being of the individual but the well-being of individuals within a wholesome community. In fact, as we read Paul's letters, we get the sense that for him the community is more important than any one individual.

As a result, the Christian life is different from both legalism, which lays down the tyranny of obeying precise rules exactly, and from libertinism, which says that anything goes without restraint.

This meant that Paul not only stood in opposition to all tendencies to reduce the Jewish Torah into legalism, but also in opposition to the spirit of Greek society. Greek society, like much of modern life, believed that all social life was based upon *eris*, which is competition and strife. That included competition and strife among individuals, among social and economic classes, among political factions, and, internationally, among city states, kingdoms, and empires. Verse 15, with its warning against biting and devouring one another, summarizes well the experience of life in classical Greece.

22

Paul's Alternative Vision

GALATIANS 5:16-26

[16] Live by the Spirit, I say, and do not gratify the desires of the flesh. [17] For what the flesh desires is opposed to the Spirit, and what the Spirit desires is opposed to the flesh; for these are opposed to each other, to prevent you from doing what you want. [18] But if you are led by the Spirit, you are not subject to the law. [19] Now the works of the flesh are obvious: fornication, impurity, licentiousness, [20] idolatry, sorcery, enmities, strife, jealousy, anger, quarrels, dissensions, factions, [21] envy, drunkenness, carousing, and things like these. I am warning you, as I warned you before: those who do such things will not inherit the kingdom of God.

[22] By contrast, the fruit of the Spirit is love, joy, peace, patience, kindness, generosity, faithfulness, [23] gentleness, and self-control. There is no law against such things. [24] And those who belong to Christ Jesus have crucified the flesh with its passions and desires. [25] If we live by the Spirit, let us also be guided by the Spirit. [26] Let us not

become conceited, competing against one another, envying one another.

HAVING LAID DOWN THE principle that what really counts is faith
working through love, Paul begins to put flesh on the bones of his
thinking. What does this Christian way of life look like?

First, he issues an imperative. "Live by the Spirit," he says,
"and do not gratify the desires of the flesh." The Greek verb that
the NRSV translates as *live* is really the word for *walk*. "Walk by the
Spirit" would be a more literal translation.

Paul shows here his Jewish upbringing. It was common in
Jewish circles to talk about the behavior of faithful people as *walking*. To walk in the way of the Lord was to behave in one's life in
accordance with the requirements of Torah. For both Judaism and
early Christianity, the life of faith was not primarily an issue of
what one believed, but of how one behaved in one's daily life. In
fact, the book of Acts tells us that the earliest name for the Christian movement was the Way.

There is an important corollary to this way of thinking about
the Christian faith. The act of faith, whether it begins with baptism or some personal commitment, say in an evangelistic meeting, does not lead one into instant transformation. It sets one on a
new road. The transformation comes as one walks faithfully down
that road. The life of faith, therefore, becomes a journey, a journey
which brings for most people a progressive transformation. Paul
has a distinct understanding of how that transformation occurs, as
we shall see in a moment.

Starting out the journey of faith also triggers a life of conflict,
an unceasing conflict between two opposing forces. Paul labels this
conflict as a conflict between the flesh and the Spirit. The desires of
the flesh, says Paul, are opposed to the Spirit, and what the Spirit
desires is opposed to the flesh. This is a conflict from which one
never escapes in this mortal life.

Now it is very tricky for modern people to read and understand what Paul is saying in the next ten verses. You recognize
that as soon as you read many biblical scholars as they maneuver
around these verses. The reason these verses are so tricky is that

we often use the words that Paul uses in different ways than Paul does. We easily import our own meanings into what Paul is saying. When we do, we get tangled in Paul's thoughts as if we are in a thorn bush thicket.

The first stumbling block is the word *flesh*. The most obvious meaning of this word is the living, soft tissue and organs that clothe the skeleton of an animal or a human being. It is the very material side of human life, something we share with all the animal world.

Americans and Europeans share a cast of thought that goes back to ancient Greek philosophers. Those ancient philosophers generally held a poor opinion of the life of the flesh. It was subject to change, disease, pain, and death. It was, therefore, not just imperfect but also corrupt in a value sense, compared to the superior life of the immaterial mind or spirit. The great object of the spiritual journey (in this Greek mind-set) was to pursue liberation from this corrupt prison of the flesh through a life of the intellect or a life of asceticism and ultimately through death.

The Hebrew Scriptures did not share this mind-set. From the creation story of Genesis 1, it was clear that not only did God create the material world, including the life of the flesh, but declared it very good.

But that material world poses a temptation to human beings. It tempts us to make the life of the flesh our primary focus in life, especially the gratifying of the desires and cravings of the flesh. We then let ourselves, our desires, and our needs become the center of the universe rather than God. This in turn leads to a disorder in our human lives, our societies, and even in the natural world beyond human beings.

So to summarize, when Paul uses the term "flesh," he is thinking of the human being as a creature of nature. As a creature of nature, we are governed by the drive for self-survival, even when that means taking the life of other living beings to sustain our own. Our orientation becomes focused on ourselves, on our own well-being and survival. The focus of our lives becomes egocentric rather than God-centered. For Paul, this is a life dominated by sin.

The desires of the flesh are opposed to the desires of the Spirit, meaning the Holy Spirit. Again, notice the choice of words Paul uses. He does not talk about the rational thoughts of the flesh or Spirit, or the philosophical principles. He talks about the desires.

The Greek word for desire that Paul uses is the word *epithumia*. It refers to those ephemeral appetites, cravings, and emotions that move us as human beings. For Paul, what ultimately drives our behavior is not our rational thoughts but our emotions, especially our longings. If you are going to change a person's behavior, you must ultimately deal with a person's feelings and not just his or her thoughts alone.

What does a life lived by the desires of the flesh look like? Well, look at its works, says Paul. And in verses 19–21, Paul lists fifteen representative vices that result from a life lived giving priority to the gratification of the desires of the flesh.

The list begins and ends with vices that any Greek or Jew would automatically associate with a life in the flesh. They include sexual immorality, alcoholic intoxication, and wanton carousing, in short, the pursuit of pleasure without restraint. One can imagine Paul's audience wagging their heads in agreement. After all, even sober pagans decried such immoderate behavior. And as new believers, Paul's audience would surely have shared his condemnation of idolatry and sorcery.

But in the middle of the list, Paul switches to talking about vices that disrupt and destroy human relationships, especially the life of communities. These include such things as enmity toward others, strife, jealousy, uncontrolled fits of anger, quarreling, factional fighting, and envy.

All of these vices are sins against the community. But we may be surprised to find that Paul lists them as works of the flesh, for all of them grow out of the longing of the flesh for one's own well-being or one's own self-vindication. They all involve a violation of the command to love our neighbor as ourselves.

A life devoted to this kind of behavior, warns Paul, will not get anyone into the kingdom of God, for the kingdom is an experience of life in which God's will for a life of love is perfectly fulfilled.

The other force in this perpetual conflict that the Christian experiences is the Holy Spirit. He is given in and through Christ. The Galatians received him when they first believed, as Paul reminded them in 3:1–5.

The result of the Holy Spirit at work in the Christian's life is what Paul calls the fruit of the Spirit. Notice that the word *fruit* is used in the singular, whereas the *works* of the flesh is in the plural. There is a hint here, I believe, that Paul sees the work of the Spirit leading Christians to an integrated life rather than to a scattered and disjointed life.

If we read carefully, we note that the fruit of the Spirit is not miracles or mighty acts of ethical behavior, but rather deep-seated traits of personal character. What the Spirit gives is not new ethical principles. What the Spirit does is nurture within us those traits of character that will express themselves naturally in the way we choose to behave.

The list of virtues, if we may call them that, begins with the virtue of love. In Greek the word used here is *agape*. It has a distinctive meaning. It does not refer to an attraction we may feel for another or warm affection we may feel for another. In fact, it does not refer primarily to a feeling. It refers to love as a basic attitude, an attitude of desiring the best welfare and well-being of another. The biblical scholar William Barclay says, "*Agape*, the Christian word, really means unconquerable benevolence."[1]

By placing the word *agape* first in the list, Paul singles out the one virtue that embraces all the others that follow. To a large degree, all the other virtues in the list fall under love's umbrella. What is important to notice, however, is that all of these virtues create space for community. Paul's chief concern in the pastoral care he extends to the church communities he founded is the welfare and unity of the whole community, and not just the welfare of scattered individuals within it.

Paul says that these two forces, the flesh and the Holy Spirit, are at war with each other in the life of the individual Christian and in the lives of churches as communities. The longings of the

1. Barclay, *Letters to the Galatians*, 54.

flesh and the longings of God's Spirit are in such opposition to each other that they constantly try to cancel each other out. This leads to a constant sense of frustration.

We must never forget this point when we are presenting the gospel to others. The gospel of Jesus Christ does indeed offer a promise of wholeness and of peace with God and other human beings, but we reach that wholeness and peace through a journey of constant conflict.

Nonetheless, Paul counsels his audience to walk by the Spirit. This points to another side of Paul's thought. Life in the Spirit is not just a passive life, one in which we do nothing but provide a clean slate on which the Spirit may write or a passive lump of clay which the Spirit may mold. We are not passive automatons of the Spirit. There is a role for us. We have a responsibility to be as deliberate as we can in walking in the ways the Spirit lays out for us, especially in cultivating and nurturing those virtues that build up rather than destroy community.

There is much more to deal with in this very dense and compact passage. I will do so in my upcoming theological reflection titled "The Spiritual Revolution in One Single Word."

23

The Bottom Line

¹ My friends, if anyone is detected in a transgression, you who have received the Spirit should restore such a one in a spirit of gentleness. Take care that you yourselves are not tempted. ² Bear one another's burdens, and in this way you will fulfill the law of Christ. ³ For if those who are nothing think they are something, they deceive themselves. ⁴ All must test their own work; then that work, rather than their neighbor's work, will become a cause for pride. ⁵ For all must carry their own loads.

⁶ Those who are taught the word must share in all good things with their teacher.

⁷ Do not be deceived; God is not mocked, for you reap whatever you sow. ⁸ If you sow to your own flesh, you will reap corruption from the flesh; but if you sow to the Spirit, you will reap eternal life from the Spirit. ⁹ So let us not grow weary in doing what is right, for we will reap at harvest-time, if we do not give up. ¹⁰ So then, whenever we have an opportunity, let us work for the good of all, and especially for those of the family of faith.

CHAPTER 5 ENDS WITH Paul's admonition to his congregations in Galatia to live and be guided in their lives by the Holy Spirit. The great corrosive of such a life is Christian elitism. Such elitism can take many forms. It can adopt an attitude that one is superior to one's fellow believers, superior because of one's ethical behavior, one's devotional practices, one's theological knowledge, one's position in the administration of the congregation, or one's physical circumcision.

Elitism inevitably moves into judgmentalism, as the "elite" Christians look down their noses at those who do not measure up to their standards. This was clearly a danger in many of the churches Paul founded. We see him deal with the problem most directly in his First Letter to the Corinthians. This may be why Paul immediately follows his admonition to be guided by the Spirit by his warning in verse 5:26 against becoming conceited and competing against and envying one another.

That admonition is a negative one. It is what living in the Spirit does *not* look like. But from a positive perspective, what does such a life look like? Paul suggests several answers in the first ten verses of chapter 6.

In the advice Paul gives, he may have been addressing specific problems in the Galatian churches. If so, his listeners would have recognized whom or what he was talking about. But he phrases his advice in more general terms, which has the benefit of making his advice more relevant to situations in other churches, including our own churches today.

First of all, life in the Spirit is not just a form of highly charged religious enthusiasm, such as we have come today to associate with some forms of Pentecostalism. Paul never devalues enthusiasm, as is clear from what he writes in First Corinthians, chapters 12–14. But Paul always subordinates enthusiasm to the higher calling of living a life that builds community. If enthusiasm tears the communal life of the congregation apart, then it is not life in the Spirit.

A key characteristic of living in a way that builds up community rather than tearing it down is bearing one another's burdens. Paul gives a concrete example of what that means in verse 6:1. If a member of the church is detected in some ethical transgression, Paul advises his or her fellow believers to correct the person with gentleness.

Paul believes in church discipline, as is clear in what he writes to the church in Corinth in the First Letter of Corinthians. But Paul is very aware of how destructive punitive judgmentalism can be in dealing with ethical lapses.

For harsh judgmentalism can add to the harm that the moral transgression has already caused. It can create a feeling of despair in the transgressor as well as creating a sense of self-righteousness among those who are doing the correcting. They easily fall into the trap that deceives them into thinking they are above such transgressions, only to find that they too are just as weak in other situations of temptation as the transgressor they are trying to correct.

Paul does not include harsh judgmentalism among the fruit of the Spirit he lists in 5:22–23. But he does list gentleness. This is wisdom that many Christians today could well pay heed to.

When Paul talks about correcting the transgressor, he gives instructions to "you who have received the Spirit." This English phrase translates a single Greek word *pneumatikoi,* which means literally *spiritual people.* Commentators have struggled with whom Paul is talking about here. Is he importing elitism in by the back door by labeling some people more spiritual than others?

We know from Paul's other letters that he recognized there were different levels of spiritual maturity present among the members of his churches. He deals with that all through his First Letter to the Corinthians. At times he urges his listeners to grow up in their faith.

But in Galatians 6:1, I don't hear Paul establishing a new, spiritual elitism in the church. First of all, as is clear from Galatians 3:2, Paul takes it for granted that all Christians have received the Spirit when they placed their faith in Christ and were baptized. So all of them are spiritual people. His advice is advice given to the whole church.

Second, if Paul has a higher level of spiritual maturity in mind, then notice how he describes it. It expresses itself in a kind of gentleness and humility in dealing with one another. If one is spiritually elite, one knows deep within one's inner being how much one is also subject to sudden lapses in ethical behavior. The spiritually mature do not compare themselves against others, but against their own inner standards and against the example set by Christ himself. Truly spiritual people will exhibit their spiritual character by serving one another in love (see Gal 5:13).

They will also take responsibility for their own lives. They will not be freeloaders depending on others to do for them what they must do for themselves. They will also not take advantage of those who teach them at great sacrifice in terms of time and money. Here, those who are taught in the fundamentals of the Christian faith and lifestyle (the Greek word means *catechized*) will support those who teach them. Although that support might involve many things, it clearly has financial support in mind.

Finally, Paul urges his listeners to do good to all people, but especially to their fellow believers in their family of faith. Paul certainly highlights the special responsibility Christians have for the well-being of their fellow believers, but it is also striking that Paul does not limit that responsibility to just fellow believers.

They are to work for the good *of all*. That would include their pagan neighbors as well as those Jews who show hostility to the Christian movement. They are not to live in isolation from the wider society. Instead, they are to work for its good. In today's language we would say the Christian call is to responsible citizenship.

Now that is remarkable advice coming from Paul when we consider that much of the wider society in which these Galatian Christians lived was hostile to their faith and lifestyle. One response could have been a withdrawal from engagement in the wider society. Christians could have retreated into defensiveness, living isolated in spiritually gated communities. Instead, Paul calls upon them to live with the risk that their engagement with the wider society will bring.

Such a way of living, as Paul describes it in these ten verses, expresses, he says, the paradoxical law of Christ. Love actually fulfills the demands of Torah. The Christian movement does not need the Jewish Torah nor to create its own Torah, for living in the Spirit means that context, not rules alone, define what is the loving act in a particular situation.

I want to acknowledge that this is a vision of the Christian life that has made Christians highly anxious through the centuries. It is a risky way to live. It does not necessarily deliver security in one's life circumstances nor certainty in one's thinking and judgment.

People can claim this rule of context as justification for all kinds of behavior that are only subtle and deceiving reassertions of sin. To protect the community against such subtle corruptions, the church through the centuries has abandoned Paul's vision, adopting all kinds of ethical prescriptions, books of discipline, canonical laws, and books of church order as protection against sin. But when we rely on such walls to protect us rather than living in the Spirit do we not fall for new, subtle expressions of the Judaizing spirit that troubled the Galatian churches?

In saying all this, we must also recognize that Paul still believes that the behavior of Christians as well as of unbelievers is important. Behavior has consequences. Many commentators believe that to make this point, Paul quotes a common proverb about our reaping whatever we sow.

If we sow to the flesh, Paul says, we will reap the harvest of the flesh, which is in part all those works of the flesh that he has described in 5:19–21. These are results that are destructive of our own well-being and the well-being of the community. The harvest of the flesh is also the fact of our physical and psychological corruption that reaches its terminus in death.

Sow instead to the Spirit. If we do, we will reap a harvest of eternal life, a life in which the fruit of the Spirit will be rich and abundant. The harvest may be slow in coming, but it will come. So do not become weary in our efforts to live by the Spirit.

Some have asked if Paul is compromising his stance that we are saved by faith. I do not hear that in his language here. Paul will always assert that we are saved by God's grace, just as Israel was liberated from Egyptian bondage by God's grace, but now that we have been set free, we have a responsibility to live a life that maintains that freedom for ourselves as well as for others. That was the original purpose of the Torah given to Israel at Sinai. And if Christians insist on developing their own Christian Torah (as we seem to do), then we must never forget that must be our purpose in doing so, too.

24

Theological Reflection
The Spiritual Revolution in One Single Word

THE LETTER TO THE Galatians has sometimes been described as the letter of the Holy Spirit. References to the Spirit occur all through the letter. It is the Spirit, not the Torah, that gives us life. It is the Spirit that liberates and transforms us.

When the Galatian Christians united themselves with Christ by faith (expressed in their baptism), they received the Spirit, says Paul. They received the Spirit by responding to the preaching of the gospel, period. They, therefore, do not need to do anything more, like adopting a Jewish Torah lifestyle, including its demand of circumcision.

This has revolutionary consequences, I believe, for how Christians think about the relation of faith and ethics/behavior in the Christian life. Christians often preach and teach that believers must express their faith in ethical or holy behavior. But the way we preach it often implies that the way we put the behavior of the Christian life into practice is by the application of our own determination and willpower. We can be obedient if we just exert enough effort to overcome the obstacles in our lives that block ethical behavior.

It was in reading Galatians, especially Galatians 5, a few years ago that I came to realize how wrong that approach is. For Paul, it is not mental determination and willpower that enable Christians to live ethical lives. Rather, it is the transforming work of the Spirit that causes ethical behavior to happen.

PAYING CLOSE ATTENTION TO THE WORDS PAUL USES

That insight came to me when I realized the import of one single word Paul uses in that famous passage of Galatians 5:22–23. That single word changed the whole way I came to understand and live the Christian life.

Let me quote those two verses again so we have them clearly before us:

> By contrast, the fruit of the Spirit is love, joy, peace, patience, kindness, generosity, faithfulness, gentleness, and self-control. There is no law against such things.

This verse falls in the passage where the Apostle Paul contrasts life in the Holy Spirit with life in the flesh. In verse 19, he lists a series of vices: fornication, impurity, licentiousness, idolatry, sorcery, enmity, strife, jealousy, anger, selfishness, dissension, party spirit, envy, drunkenness, and carousing. He calls these vices "works of the flesh."

He contrasts these with what he calls the *fruit* of the Spirit. Now what caught my attention is that he calls these Christian virtues *fruit* of the Spirit, not *works* of the Spirit. I expected him to write *works*. That would be expected if he were trying for a parallelism in his wording. So why does he write *fruit* instead? That was the question I asked myself.

I suspect he used *fruit* instead of *works* because the word *works* can be misleading. It suggests that these virtues are something we must work hard to acquire or express in our life. Using the word *works* would incline us to put our focus on what we do. That in turn would feed scrupulosity or guilty feelings as we try to live out these virtues and fail over and over again. We would make our Christians lives an exhausting and frustrating affair. That is how I once read this passage. I felt these virtues were something I had to work hard at acquiring. The legalistic spirit of the Christianity in which I was raised fed this feeling in a mighty way. It produced a fruit of bitterness and indeed exhaustion.

But that is not what Paul is saying. He is not saying these virtues are a result of our hard work. They are the result of the Holy Spirit's work in our lives. They are the fruit or by-product of living a deeply spiritual life.

The apricots on an apricot tree are the end result of the growth process of the tree. If the tree is healthy, if it is planted in good soil and fertilized and well watered, it will ultimately produce its apricots as a result of the life forces of the tree rising in the tree and producing its flowers and then its fruit.

If the tree is healthy, it will produce good fruit. If it is diseased, it will produce no fruit or diseased fruit. This is the point that Jesus too makes in the Sermon on the Mount in Matthew 7:15–20. Jesus and Paul are at one in their viewpoint.

PAUL VERSUS THE GREEKS: WHAT IS THE KEY TO ETHICAL BEHAVIOR?

I see Paul (and Jesus) running in a diametrically opposite direction to much of Greek philosophy in his own day, the Greek philosophy that lies behind much of our thinking about ethics even today. Greek philosophy generally took the stance that if we could come to know the good, we would live out the good. The key to ethical behavior is knowledge. Knowing inevitably leads to doing. If I understand Socrates right, that was his fundamental conviction. It is why he spent his life in dialogue with others seeking to get a vision or understanding of the good.

That is not the viewpoint of Paul, if we listen carefully to what he says in Galatians 5:16–17:

> Live by the Spirit, I say, and do not gratify the desires
> of the flesh. For what the flesh desires is opposed to the
> Spirit, and what the Spirit desires is opposed to the flesh;
> for these are opposed to each other, to prevent you from
> doing what you want.

Notice in these verses the repeated use of the word *desires*. Paul, I think, operates from the understanding that desires, not knowledge, ultimately drive our action. The problem with ethical behavior, therefore, is not knowledge, but the inner motivation of the heart. Over and over again, we show that we know what the good is, but we can't live it out because we do not want to. The key to ethical behavior is changing our inner desires.

For Paul, changing the inner heart is not something we do by deliberate willpower, but something that happens to us through the impact of other forces in our lives. For the Christian, that change comes from the impact of the Holy Spirit at work in our inner being.

The author of 1 John shares Paul's conviction that the key to ethical behavior is a transformation of the inner desires, but for him this comes by our truly experiencing the love of God in our lives. "We love because he [God] first loved us" (1 John 4:19).

We change Christian behavior not by preaching hellfire and damnation, by lengthy, emotional exhortations, nor by detailed ethical discourses. Such techniques may trigger feelings of guilt. That guilt can temporarily cause people to change how they act, but they do not change the inner heart, which is the key to changing long-term behavior.

The secret to producing those virtues Paul calls the fruit of the Spirit is not our hard work, our exhausting work to produce these virtues by acts of sheer willpower. No, the secret is to root our lives in the Holy Spirit. As we seek to lay down roots in the Holy Spirit, the Spirit will begin to work in our inner lives to transform our motivations, our desires, and our mind-sets. As those motivations, desires, and mind-sets change, our behavior will follow.

What we need to preach is the need to open our lives to the work of the Holy Spirit. We are changed as we immerse ourselves in the life of the Spirit.

TAPPING INTO THE LIVING WATER OF THE SPIRIT

It is amazing to see how consistent Paul is in his thinking with others in the biblical record. We have already noted what Jesus says in the Sermon on the Mount.

We need to note as well the preaching of John the Baptist as reported in the gospels. They tell us that John preached a message of repentance for the forgiveness of sins. This repentance was initiated in the act of baptism. Yet John was well aware that his baptism would not transform the inner heart, for he also preaches, "I have baptized you with water, but he [the greater one who will come after him] will baptize with Holy Spirit" (Mark 1:8). That baptism is a far greater baptism.

We can also link Galatians 5:22–23 to Psalm 1. In the psalm, we have the image of a righteous person as a sturdy, mature tree that is well rooted by streams of water. It stands firm in the many storms that life brings. It produces its fruit in due season.

What is the secret of its stability and fruitfulness? It is that the righteous person roots himself or herself into a daily meditation upon the Torah of God. The psalmist is not advocating a legalistic lifestyle, but a meditative reading of Scripture as he knows it.

Jesus picks up this image of streams of water and sees it as an image of the Holy Spirit (see John 7:37–39).

What Paul would have us do is not work so hard at trying to achieve the virtues of the Christian life. He would have us work hard at rooting ourselves in the Spirit. If we work hard at becoming more and more open to the Spirit in our lives, the Spirit will transform us.

THE VITAL ROLE OF THE SPIRITUAL DISCIPLINES

The question that arises at this point is how we open our lives to the Spirit. Here we come to the importance of those spiritual practices that have become known in Christian spirituality as the spiritual disciplines. All of those disciplines are aimed at opening our lives to the transforming work of the Spirit.

One of those disciplines is regular participation in the worship life of our church. Just attending church routinely may not carry us very far into spiritual maturity. One need only point to the many spiritually immature people sitting in our church pews. But there is still something to be said for regularly showing up, for, as Paul will make clear in other places in his letters, it is in the church as the community of faith that the Holy Spirit works. We expose ourselves to the Spirit as we participate in the church's worship. And no one can say how the Spirit may use that exposure to advance his work within us.

Other disciplines are time-honored in Christian practice. They include:

- *Prayer in all its forms.* It is my personal conviction that if we would live a vital Christian life, we must live and breathe in a sea of prayer just as a fish swims in the ocean. That's how essential prayer is to life in the Spirit. For myself, the most productive form of prayer in cultivating the fruit of the Spirit has been the practice of contemplative prayers of silence. In silence, we have a way of letting go of our own agendas in terms of our thoughts, feelings, and desires and just being with God without any demands. Contemplative prayer is a great tool for taming our basic egocentrism.

- *Bible reading*, especially that form of meditative reading that is called lectio divina (divine reading). This is a practice which turns Bible reading into a form of prayer. It lies at the heart of monastic spirituality as it does as well in the hallowed Protestant practice of a "quiet time with Scripture."

- *The practice of hospitality.* In welcoming others, we never know what insights and gifts of healing the Spirit may bring us through our conversations and interactions with others, especially strangers. The classic example in Scripture is found in Genesis 18, where Abraham and Sarah entertain three strangers by the oak of Mamre. In this story, the roles of hosts and guests become reversed as Abraham and Sarah receive an unexpected blessing from their guests.

- *Sabbath keeping.* Setting aside time to drop our work activities and our obsessions not only refreshes us in body, mind, and spirit, but also creates space for the Spirit to act in our lives in unexpected ways. Being *with* God becomes more important than anything we do. The time does not have to be Sunday; we can stop for Sabbath times of rest all through the week.

- *The practice of the presence of God.* In this practice we punctuate all our daily activities with short, ejaculatory prayers invoking the presence of God into that very moment of our daily routines. The great exponent of this practice was Brother Lawrence, a seventeenth-century French monk. He made it his daily practice. As a result, he said, he felt the presence of God with him just as much when he was busy in his kitchen (he was the monastery's cook) as when he knelt in prayer in the chapel.

- *Regular and frequent participation in the sacraments,* especially the Eucharist (the Lord's Supper). At dark moments in my own spiritual life, nothing has been so powerful in communicating to me the profound love of God as participation in the Eucharist. When the minister hands to me the physical bread and wine, I have often had the sensation of God feeding me as a father feeds his infant. It has been profoundly transformative for me.

- *Joining with other Christians in serving others.* As we walk in the footsteps of Christ in service, we align ourselves with him. If we love because God first loved us, as 1 John says, one of the most profound ways we can open our lives to the Holy Spirit is by experiencing love freely given and received in the community of believers. Paul puts it in Galatians 6:2: "Bear one another's burdens and so fulfill the law of Christ."

- *Standing up and working for justice.* We also align ourselves with Christ and the Holy Spirit when we take a stand for justice or join with others in working for it. I once heard a person put it succinctly. "When I walk in a protest march," he said, "my feet become a form of prayer." There's an important truth in his words. Our actions constitute prayer just as much as our words. The Spirit can use such actions to work transformation both within us and within the wider society.

I could go on. There are many other disciplines that Christians have practiced through the centuries. In all of them we are given an opportunity to unite ourselves with Christ in deeper ways, so the Holy Spirit can be given an opening to work in our lives and transform our inner desires. As the Spirit does so, our lives come to naturally express the virtues to which God calls us.

THE FRUIT OF THE SPIRIT AS TRAITS OF CHARACTER

There is one more thing to notice about the fruit of the Spirit as Paul lists it in Galatians 5:22–23. Everything he lists is not an action of ours. Instead, they are traits of character, qualities of character that especially build community.

This has another important consequence. What is the convincing proof of the presence of the Holy Spirit in a Christian's life or in a church community? For Paul, it is not spectacular miracles or mystical experiences, even though he believes in and has experienced them. No, it is the presence of the fruit of the Spirit . . . the presence of love, joy, peace, patience, kindness, goodness, faithfulness, gentleness, and self-control. Where such fruit is manifest, there we know the Holy Spirit is at work.

When all the implications of what Paul is saying dawned within my consciousness, it turned my religious life upside down. Instead of spending so much energy trying to be good, I found I was called to spend my energy trying to become more open to the Spirit.

I may be far from perfect in expressing Paul's fruit of the Spirit in my way of living. But I don't worry about that much. If I am faithful in working to become open to the Spirit in my life, those virtues will come, just as the apricot grows on the apricot tree. The fruit of the Spirit is the by-product of living a spiritual life; it is not life's primary focus. "Seek first God's kingship and his righteousness, and all these things shall be yours as well," says Jesus in the Sermon on the Mount (Matt 6:33). "All these things" includes the virtues of the Christian life as well as the physical and material necessities of life.

GOD AT WORK IN OUR ACTIONS

This is not to say that the Christian life is a purely passive affair, where we just lie back and let God do all the work. If we read Paul in that way, we misread him. Just two verses later in Galatians, Paul will also say, "If we live by the Spirit, let us also walk by the Spirit" (Gal 5:25).

We have a responsibility to try to live out these virtues as best we can. We try to walk the way we talk. But our actions in essence become a kind of prayer. By our efforts we appeal to God to work that transformation within us where these virtues become natural expressions of who we are and what we are becoming, new creations in Christ. What Paul has in mind is better captured, I believe, in another of his letters, in Philippians 2:5–13:

> Let the same mind be in you that was in Christ Jesus,
> who, though he was in the form of God,
> did not regard equality with God
> as something to be exploited,
> but emptied himself,
> taking the form of a slave,

being born in human likeness.
And being found in human form,
he humbled himself
and became obedient to the point of death—
even death on a cross.

Therefore God also highly exalted him
and gave him the name
that is above every name,
so that at the name of Jesus
every knee should bend,
in heaven and on earth and under the earth,
and every tongue should confess
that Jesus Christ is Lord,
to the glory of God the Father.

Therefore, my beloved, just as you have always obeyed me, not only in my presence, but much more now in my absence, work out your own salvation with fear and trembling; for it is God who is at work in you, enabling you both to will and to work for his good pleasure.

This passage is one of the great christological statements in the New Testament. Paul urges us to adopt the mind of Christ, and the mind of Christ is set before us in the way Jesus lived, died, and rose again. But notice how Paul draws the consequence of this for the way we Christians should live.

Paul calls us to *work out* your salvation, yet, paradoxically, Paul says, it is God who is at work in you, to *will* and *work* for his good pleasure. We have responsibilities, but as we exercise those responsibilities, God works with us to will (or desire) his good pleasure, and God gives us the power to express those transformed desires into action. The result is not pride in our accomplishments, but a feeling of humility and gratitude toward God.

This is the paradox of the life to which the Christian gospel calls us.

THE HOPE FOR ULTIMATE TRANSFORMATION

The transformation the Holy Spirit works in our lives is never complete in this life. The flesh and the Spirit are in constant tension in this life, so the Christian life involves an incessant struggle (Gal 5:17). We live in constant tension as the *desires* of the flesh and the *desires* of the Spirit war against each other. But the Christian hope is that the transformation will be complete someday, when not only we, but all creation will be fully transformed by the Holy Spirit.

Paul expresses this hope in a famous passage in Romans 8:18–24:

> I consider that the sufferings of this present time are not worth comparing with the glory about to be revealed to us. For the creation waits with eager longing for the revealing of the children of God; for the creation was subjected to futility, not of its own will but by the will of the one who subjected it, in hope that the creation itself will be set free from its bondage to decay and will obtain the freedom of the glory of the children of God. We know that the whole creation has been groaning in labor pains until now; and not only the creation, but we ourselves, who have the first fruits of the Spirit, groan inwardly while we wait for adoption, the redemption of our bodies. For in hope we were saved. Now hope that is seen is not hope. For who hopes for what is seen?

All creation, Paul says, will be freed from bondage to decay and corruption, and from its fight for self-survival, and will enjoy the freedom of the sons of God. Once again, Paul has a profoundly different understanding of what God is doing in Christ.

Here's how I appropriate this for myself. In the world we know (the world Paul will call the world of the flesh), evolution guides development. Through long stages, evolution arrives at human beings. But the question arises: Does evolution stop with human beings? Or is there yet a higher life form to evolve out of man?

I think Paul might suggest the answer is Yes. The next step in the evolutionary process is the transformation of egocentric human beings into God-centered beings who are filled with the Holy Spirit, indeed beings who are human, yet in some way are indwelt by God himself. Such a step would be nothing short than a new creation.

Paul says that in Christ, that new creation has arrived on earth. And as we are united with Christ, we experience ourselves entering into it.

In this vision, the Old Testament Torah has its place. It was to lead humanity up to Christ. But with the arrival of Christ and the accomplishment of his redemptive mission in the cross, a new creation has also arrived, a new creation in which all humanity has the potential of being filled with the Holy Spirit and living by the Holy Spirit.

In the book of Revelation, this is seen symbolically by the creation of a new earth where there is no temple because God dwells with human beings (Rev 21:22). In Eastern Orthodox theology, this vision is expressed in the phrase, "God became a human being in order than we might be made divine." In this Christian vision of the future, material creation is not escaped or abandoned (as in Platonism or Hinduism), but material creation is transformed by the resurrection of the body.

In this new creation, the Christmas promise of Emmanuel (God with us) receives its ultimate and astonishing fulfillment.

25

A Concluding Subscript

GALATIANS 6:11–18

[11] See what large letters I make when I am writing in my own hand! [12] It is those who want to make a good showing in the flesh that try to compel you to be circumcised—only that they may not be persecuted for the cross of Christ. [13] Even the circumcised do not themselves obey the law, but they want you to be circumcised so that they may boast about your flesh. [14] May I never boast of anything except the cross of our Lord Jesus Christ, by which the world has been crucified to me, and I to the world. [15] For neither circumcision nor uncircumcision is anything; but a new creation is everything! [16] As for those who will follow this rule—peace be upon them, and mercy, and upon the Israel of God.

[17] From now on, let no one make trouble for me; for I carry the marks of Jesus branded on my body.

[18] May the grace of our Lord Jesus Christ be with your spirit, brothers and sisters. Amen.

FROM VARIOUS THINGS PAUL says in other letters, we get some glimpse of how Paul wrote his letters to his churches. He did not sit down at a table and pick up pen and ink to draft his own letter. Instead, his practice was to dictate his letters to a secretary, who wrote his words down on the papyrus sheets.

That is clearly what Paul was doing in drafting his Letter to the Galatian churches. We glimpse this in verse 11, where Paul alludes to the large letters he makes when he writes with his own hand. This implies that he did not personally write down all that preceded this. His secretary wrote it down.

But now that the Letter to the Galatians is complete, Paul picks up the pen from his secretary and adds a personal subscript to the letter, his own personal P.S.

Either his handwriting was much bigger than his secretary's or he wanted to make sure his audience did not miss the import of what he had to say in these final sentences, for what he does is make one final assertion of his basic theological point all through the letter. What is important is not circumcision or uncircumcision, but the transformed life the Galatian believers are living and are called to live. It is a life transformed from a life lived by the desires of the flesh into a life lived by the motivating power of the Holy Spirit.

So dramatic and extraordinary is this transformation that Paul calls it a new creation. They are entering into a new universe created by God, not by God's abolition and destruction of the old universe, but by God's transforming power. The old universe of the flesh is being transformed into one in which flesh is fulfilled and redeemed by its union with the Spirit.

Paul has not used this language of new creation in the Letter to the Galatians previously. But it is not a stray or fleeting feature of his thinking. In 2 Corinthians 5:17, Paul also calls attention to this new creation in a striking verse that reads, "So if anyone is in Christ, there is a new creation: everything old has passed away; see, everything has become new!"

It is easy for Christians to assume that the Christian gospel is all about God saving each of us as individuals so that we can go to heaven when we die. Certainly God is concerned with the eternal welfare of each individual person in the world and in each generation of human history. But if we settle for such an understanding of the gospel, we are, in my opinion, settling for a constricted and anemic gospel.

The Christian gospel is about a big, big story. It is about nothing less than the coming of a new creation, a transformed creation that includes not only human beings but a transformation of all of the natural world around us, a transformation that extends to and embraces the billions upon billions of galaxies that compose our universe and all the infinitesimal atomic processes that undergird them.

We glimpse the vastness of Paul's vision in passages like Ephesians 1:9–11 and Colossians 1:15–20. In these passages Paul regards the fulfillment of God's redemptive purposes in Jesus Christ to be none other than the gathering up of all things, in heaven and in earth, and their unification in Christ as lord of the cosmos.

This is a vision that should take our breath away, for this is a vision of nothing less than a new creation. As Revelation 21:1 also puts it, "Then I saw a new heavens and a new earth; for the first heaven and the first earth had passed away, and the sea was no more."

If we do not include this breathtaking vision of God's purpose in our preaching of the gospel, then we do not do justice to the good news, for that story is much bigger and more awesome than just the eternal destiny of each one of us as individuals.

This vision of the future helps put into perspective the harassment and persecution that the Galatian Christians experienced just as Paul himself experienced them. What initiated this new creation that God brought about was the crucifixion of Jesus, which is what Paul has in mind when he talks about the cross of Christ.[1]

In the crucifixion, Jesus lived and died by a completely different standard than the law of self-survival that rules in both the

---

1. Although in these verses Paul speaks exclusively of the crucifixion of Christ, this does not mean he denies or subordinates the resurrection. As we see in other letters of his, especially 1 Corinthians 15 and 2 Corinthians 5, the resurrection is the other side of this great redemptive act of God. But the crucifixion has particular significance for Paul because it was such a scandalous part of the gospel for both nonbelieving Jews and pagans.

natural world and in the cultural world of humanity. He lived and died by the standard of complete trust in the God he called Father. When Christians place their trust in this Christ and are united with him in baptism, they come to share in this experience of being crucified to the natural, social, and cultural world in which they live, as Paul says he himself has been. Now their—and his—significance are found in Christ, for in Christ they are one with one another.

This means that all the identity markers of life in this world—physical markers like circumcision, tattoos, skin color, or gender, and social/cultural markers like language, cultural taboos, social class, and national/tribal histories—have been subordinated to this new identity of oneness that they all possess in Christ. Those identity markers do not vanish in this life. But they no longer dictate that some people are treated with more or less respect than others.

For Paul, the trouble with his Judaizing opponents is that they do not yet understand what a radical break the crucifixion and resurrection of Jesus have made with all those identity markers that govern human life. They see those markers continuing to be valid in their new life in Christ.

They do so, Paul asserts, from faulty motivations. On the one hand, they are seeking to avoid persecution. What Paul seems to be suggesting here is that Judaizing Christians were seeking to evade persecution from nonbelieving Jews by showing that Gentile Christians accepted circumcision and were therefore essentially Jewish proselytes. And if they were proselytes, then these new Gentile Christians offered no threat to Judaism with its priority on Torah.

On the other hand, the Judaizing Christians may have sought to establish their prestige among their fellow Jews and Jewish-Christians by showing how they brought this harvest of Gentile converts into the Jewish barn.

But Paul will have none of this. "For," he writes, "neither circumcision or uncircumcision is anything; but a new creation is everything." This is the new rule of faith in the Christian movement.

Upon all those who follow this new rule of faith, Paul pronounces a blessing of peace.

Paul then closes his Letter to the Galatians with a second blessing. He wishes upon them the grace of our Lord Jesus Christ. Here he invokes the name of Jesus in its most solemn and sublime liturgical form: our Lord Jesus Christ.

The essence of his wish is the wish for grace, for in the end what Paul's gospel is all about is a message of God's grace, God's loving favor upon all humankind, God being *for* us despite all that suggests otherwise. On this truth we can trust and so live.

The last words of the letter, apart from the word *Amen*, are "brothers and sisters." The Letter to the Galatians has been filled with harsh criticism, some bitter rebukes, and occasionally some intemperate language. But in the end it has been all motivated by Paul's love and deep concern for the spiritual well-being of the churches he founded. He signals that by closing the letter on a note of his sense of affection and family relationship with the Galatian Christians.

If we have followed along with Paul in this complex letter and have come to understand something of the awesome vision he sets before us, we too will join with him in saying *Amen*.

26

Theological Reflection
Who Is the Israel of God?

AT THE CONCLUSION OF the Letter to the Galatians, Paul extends two blessings on his listeners. One is a wish for peace, expressed in Galatians 6:16. He extends it to all who follow the rule of faith he has expressed in the previous sentence. The second is a concluding blessing in Galatians 6:18. It is the final sentence of the letter. In it, Paul extends a wish for the grace of the Lord Jesus Christ to rest upon all his brothers and sisters in the churches of Galatia.

Both blessings seek to be irenic notes on which to end this letter of controversy and stern rebuke. But, ironically, the first blessing has been a source of intense debate.

Let us get the blessing before us in the translation adopted by the NRSV. I will quote not only verse 16 but also verse 15 on which it hangs:

> For neither circumcision nor uncircumcision is any-
> thing; but a new creation is everything! As for those who
> will follow this rule—peace be upon them, and mercy,
> and upon the Israel of God.

THE CHALLENGE OF TRANSLATION

The question is how to best translate verse 16. In ancient manuscripts, scribes customarily used no punctuation in writing sentences or paragraphs. So in the early manuscripts, if we were to translate the verse literally without any punctuation, it would read, "Peace upon them and mercy and upon the Israel of God." Translators have to decide how to punctuate it when translating it into English.

How they decide to punctuate it depends upon how they understand what Paul is saying. One way is to understand the phrase "Israel of God" as referring to the Christian church. In that case, then Paul is wishing peace and mercy on them who are the Christian church. They are the true Israel of God.

Another way to understand the phrase is to understand *them* as referring to those who follow the rule of faith he has articulated. On them he wishes peace. The Israel of God, however, refers to the non-Christian Jewish people. On them (*and* then means *in addition*) Paul wishes God's mercy. The translators of the NRSV seem to understand it this way. The phrase then becomes a kind of irenic gesture toward nonbelieving Jews.

There is a third way to understand it. This is the way I prefer. The phrase "Israel of God" is an odd choice of words. It is never used in the Hebrew Old Testament, nor is it used anywhere else in the New Testament, including Paul's other writings.

But throughout the argument of Galatians, the question Paul tries to answer is: Who are the children of Abraham, father of Israel? They include, Paul says, believing Gentiles as well as believing Jews. They are the children of the free woman, as Paul says in Galatians 4:31. Presumably they both form the Israel of God.

But maybe that includes nonbelieving Jews as well. From what Paul writes in Romans 9–11, we learn Paul expects that someday nonbelieving Jews will also be included in the people of God at the end of time. The phrase "Israel of God" then becomes ambiguously but radically inclusive. Its very ambiguity bears witness to a mystery in God's redemptive action that is not fully clear to us at this time.

WHY THE TRANSLATION MATTERS

Why belabor these translation options? Because this phrase has sometimes been used to argue that the Christian church supplants Judaism as the true people of God. This doctrine is given the name supersessionism. It states that with the coming of Christ, the Christian church superseded ethnic Israel as the chosen, covenant people of God.

This doctrine has fed a great deal of Christian anti-Semitism. It has encouraged the idea that God rejected and discarded the Jews, and therefore so can Christians. One fruit of this doctrine is the long, ugly history of Christian persecution of Jews, which saw its most horrifying expression in the Holocaust during World War II.

Translation option number one as I listed above seems to understand Paul's odd phrase in this supersessionist way. If we adopt it as the correct translation, then we must do so acknowledging the ugly fruit Paul's blessing has borne.

But I personally find it hard to believe that Paul, despite all his debate with his fellow Jews, would sanction the kind of anti-Semitism that some Christians have drawn from this verse in Galatians. It goes against the grain of what Paul says in Romans 9:1–5 about his willingness to be accursed and cut off from Christ if that would help bring his fellow Jews into Christ. This is not the language of hatred. It is the language of impassioned love.

I opt for translation option number three, for I believe it is more consistent with Paul's vision as revealed not only in Galatians, but in his other letters, especially in Romans 11:25–32. There, Paul says that a hardening (of heart or mind) has come upon a part of ethnic Israel so that Gentiles may come into the household of faith. But in the end, all Israel will be saved. He draws from this the conclusion that "God has imprisoned all in disobedience so that he may be merciful to all."

AN INCLUSIVE VISION

We cannot say whether Paul is teaching universal salvation, but he certainly is laying before us a very inclusive vision, a vision that embraces both Jews and Gentiles in the people of God. When we combine this vision with what Paul says about God gathering up all things in heaven and earth in Christ (see Eph 1:9–10), and reconciling in Christ all things, whether in heaven or on earth (see Col 1:20), we begin to glimpse the breathtaking vision Paul holds out to us. God's plan is to unite all things and all people in Christ.

No one, I believe, has ever expressed this vision quite as dazzlingly as the poet Dante in the final cantos of his *Divine Comedy.* There he is given a vision of Paradise. In this vision, rank upon rank of the redeemed rise and form the petals of a vast, cosmic rose, all focused on the rose's center, the Triune God enclosed in radiant light. Here the powers of imagination fail him in his efforts to describe the ineffable vision.

These ranks of the redeemed in Dante's vision are, I contend, the true people of God to whom Paul and the whole of the biblical witness would have us direct our attention. And so in respect to Jews and all the peoples of the world, I believe we need to understand Paul's Israel of God not narrowly, but generously. To God be the glory!

27

A Final Comment

IF WHAT I HAVE been expounding in this study guide is an accurate interpretation of Paul, then I hope you may begin to understand why Paul's Letter to the Galatians has exercised such extraordinary power in the life of the church over the centuries. It profoundly transformed the thinking of Martin Luther and through Luther helped spark the Protestant Reformation. It has revolutionized my own thinking about the Christian life, especially as I think about the role of the Holy Spirit in the individual Christian's life as well as in the life of the Christian church.

In conclusion, I want to quote the theologian Richard Longenecker, who says this on the importance of the Letter to the Galatians:

> Historically, Paul's Letter to the Galatians has been foundational for many forms of Christian thought, proclamation, and practice. Likewise, today, how one understands the issues and teaching of Galatians determines in large measure what kind of theology one espouses, what kind of message one proclaims, and what kind of lifestyle one lives.[1]

1. Longenecker, *Galatians*, 301.

I invite you to immerse yourself in the Letter to the Galatians and see where Paul—and the Holy Spirit—lead you. You may be surprised.

For Further Study

IF YOU WISH TO study the Letter to the Galatians in greater depth or explore alternate perspectives on Paul's work, there is a wealth of resources available to you. If one were to collect all the commentaries and academic treatises written on Galatians as well as other study guides and articles, the collection would compose an extensive library in itself.

Here are a few resources that have enriched my own study. Some are academic; others are targeted to the lay reader. But on the whole, all of them should be accessible to a layperson wanting to explore Paul's letter in greater detail.

Barclay, William. *The Letters to the Galatians and Ephesians.* New Daily Study Bible. Louisville: Westminster John Knox, 2002.

Barclay, a Church of Scotland minister and scholar, wrote commentaries on all the books of the New Testament. Many today find them dated, but I still recommend them for three reasons. (1) He is always very readable. (2) He has a superb command of New Testament Greek. He opens up the cultural context of many Greek words in the text. (3) He can be inspirational for pastors and teachers who seek to apply the Biblical text to life today.

Betz, Hans Dieter. "Galatians, Epistle to the." In *The Anchor Bible Dictionary*, edited by David Noel Freedman, 2:872–75. New York: Doubleday, 1992.

This short dictionary entry on the Letter to the Galatians offers a succinct summary of the many scholarly issues involved in interpreting Galatians. It is a good place for a lay teacher to find a brief orientation to the letter.

Brown, Raymond E. *An Introduction to the New Testament.* 1st ed. Anchor Yale Bible Reference Library. New York: Doubleday, 1997.

Brown offers an excellent introduction to a serious study of the New Testament. He is especially accessible to students who have no or little background in Bible study. His chapter on Galatians not only provides background for reading the letter, but also alerts the reader to some of the issues scholars still debate over interpretation.

Cousar, Charles B. *Galatians.* Interpretation: A Bible Commentary for Teaching and Preaching. Louisville: Westminster John Knox, 1982.

This commentary series is targeted to both preachers and lay Bible teachers. It superbly blends exegesis with theological discussion of how the text speaks to us today.

Dunn, James D. G. *The Epistle to the Galatians.* Black's New Testament Commentary. London: A. & C. Black, 1993.

Dunn provides a line-by-line exegesis of every sentence and word in Galatians. He often discusses the meaning of the original Greek, but his discussion really focuses on the English text. I find him very helpful.

Johnson, Luke Timothy. "Lecture 8: Life and Law—Galatians."
Apostle Paul, lecture series. The Great Courses, 2001. http://
www.thegreatcourses.com/courses/apostle-paul.html.

This is a twelve-part audio/video lecture series produced by the
Great Courses. Johnson is always a stimulating lecturer. His lecture
will appeal to lay people by providing background on the situation
Paul addresses in the letter. It also gives a broad overview of Paul's
argument in the letter.

Levine, Amy-Jill, and Marc Zvi Brettler, eds. The Jewish Annotated
New Testament. Oxford: Oxford University Press, 2011.

This is a very useful resource in studying Galatians, for two reasons. (1) Jewish scholar Shaye J. D. Cohen provides exegetical
notes to Galatians that read the letter from a Jewish perspective.
(2) At the end of the volume come eighteen essays in which Jewish
scholars discuss various aspects of Jewish life and thought in the
first century when Paul was writing. Christians often misunderstand the Jewish context in which the New Testament arose. These
essays provide a helpful corrective.

Longenecker, Richard N. Galatians. Word Biblical Commentary
41. Nashville: Thomas Nelson, 1990.

Longenecker provides detailed exegesis on the Greek text. His
book is filled with scholarly detail and citations that may exhaust a
lay teacher, but it is very good if one wants to explore such detail as
one prepares to teach Galatians to a lay audience.

Luther, Martin. Commentary on Galatians. Translated by Erasmus
Middleton. Edited by John Prince Fallowes. Grand Rapids:
Kregel, 1979.

In his commentary published in 1523, Martin Luther reads Galatians as espousing salvation by faith versus salvation by works.
It set the fundamental approach to most Protestant interpretation
of Galatians until very recent times. If you wish to understand the

source of this interpretation, you will want to immerse yourself in Luther's commentary.

Soards, Marion L., and Darrell J. Pursiful. *Galatians*. Smyth & Helwys Bible Commentary 26A. Macon, GA: Smyth & Helwys, 2015.

This commentary tries to draw upon the best in academic work on Galatians, but make it accessible to readers outside the theological profession. It will, however, make demands on a lay reader who chooses to tackle it. What is noteworthy in this commentary is that it includes a CD that allows readers to access background material, images, maps, and other online study resources.

Wright, N. T. *Paul for Everyone: Galatians and Thessalonians*. Louisville: Westminster John Knox, 2002.

Wright is a renowned New Testament scholar, especially on Paul. He has written extensively on first-century Jewish and Greco-Roman life and the New Testament text. This particular volume is a short commentary primarily targeted to the lay reader. It gives a condensed guide to the letters, which will be useful for someone who wants a light introduction to the Letter to the Galatians. For a more in-depth discussion, you will need to turn to his other books.

Wright, N. T. "The Letter to the Galatians: Exegesis and Theology." In *Between Two Horizons: Spanning New Testament Studies and Systematic Theology*, edited by Joel B. Green and Max Turner, 205–36. Grand Rapids: Eerdmans, 2000.

This article gives a more extensive discussion of Wright's view on the exegetical and theological issues we encounter in reading Galatians. Available at http://ntwrightpage.com/2016/07/12/the-letter-to-the-galatians-exegesis-and-theology/.

Works Cited

Barclay, William. *The Letters to the Galatians and Ephesians.* Daily Study Bible. Philadelphia: Westminster, 1954.

Book of Order: The Constitution of the Presbyterian Church (USA), Part II, 2007–2009. Louisville: Office of the General Assembly, 2007.

Dunn, James D. G. *The Epistle to the Galatians.* Black's New Testament Commentary. London: A. & C. Black, 1993.

Herbermann, Charles G., et al., eds. *Catholic Encyclopedia.* New York: Encyclopedia Press, 1913. Published online by New Advent. http://www.newadvent.org/cathen.

Longenecker, Richard N. *Galatians.* Word Biblical Commentary 41. Nashville: Thomas Nelson, 1990.